Landmarks

GRAMMAR ■ USAGE ■ MECHANICS

CAMBRIDGE BOOK COMPANY
488 Madison Avenue
New York, N.Y. 10022

A NEW YORK TIMES COMPANY

Layout and design by Walter A. Schwarz

Credits: p. 5, courtesy Popofsky Advertising; p. 30, courtesy Western Electric; p. 39, courtesy American Cancer Society, International Ladies Garment Workers Union, Warner-Lambert Company, The Woolbureau, Inc.; pp. 50-51 New York Public Library, courtesy of Perfection in Performance, Inc., courtesy of CBS Television; p. 56 and p. 121 Museum of Modern Art Film Stills Archive; p. 77 courtesy Roosevelt Island Development Corporation; p. 105, courtesy Corning Glass Works; p. 149 courtesy Pentalic Corporation; other photos, The New York Times.

Copyright © 1976 by Cambridge Book Company, a division of the New York Times Media Co., Inc. All rights reserved. No part of this work covered by the copyrights hereon may be reproduced or used in any form or by any means—graphic, electronic, or mechanical, including photocopying, recording, taping or information storage and retrieval systems—without written permission of the publisher. Manufactured in the United States of America.

Landmarks

Sister Agnes Ann Pastva, S.N.D.
Department of English, Cleveland Diocesan School System, Cleveland, Ohio

Contents

What's in a Name?	1
Resources	35
Whodunit?	56
Underpinnings	77
In Agreement	102
Capitalization	124
The End of the Line	133
If You Can't Spell It . . .	162
Index to Usage and Style	177

Introduction

Read this sentence (?):

> Heart the springs song often from.

Something is very wrong here. Probably you've heard the old taboo that a sentence should never end with a preposition. Since *from* is a preposition, maybe that's what's wrong with this sentence. If you place the preposition first you have

> From heart the springs song often.

In English you may *learn by heart,* yet you never hear the expression *from heart.* What word would you put between? No one has to tell you that *from the heart* sounds better. Now you have

> From the heart springs song often.

What other word-position changes would you recommend to force this sentence to make sense?

If you juggle a bit, you will probably conclude that

> Song often springs from the heart.

is the best arrangement.

How did you arrive at these decisions? The fact is you've been arranging words to make sense to those around you from the time you began to talk. You don't need to study word order because you've been an expert word-juggler for so long now. This book won't explain in detail things about English that you already know. Instead it will concentrate on those things that may puzzle or even confuse you when you try to express your ideas in the hardest way of all—in writing.

TO KILL A CHICKENHAWK

BUTCHERSHOP-FIVE

WHAT'S IN A NAME?

Jonathan Lorenzo Seagull

THE PITCHER IN THE RYE

Would you pick up a book with the title *The Locust Years*? Or choose *The Little I* from the library shelf? Chances are that you have read at least one of these books.

The title of a book is often the first reason you are interested in reading it. These two names were the original titles for *The Chosen* and *I Never Promised You a Rose Garden*. Can you guess the final titles for *Tomorrow Is Another Day* and *Gold-Hatted Gatsby*?

Book titles are just one indication of the importance of word choices. Before you can make the right word choice, you must be sure of basic meanings.

Synonyms

Which of the four words in each group is *not* a synonym?

1. death, mystery, enigma, puzzle
2. query, question, strange, interrogation
3. fight, conflict, loss, battle
4. grief, sorrow, numbness, sadness
5. perplex, puzzle, mystify, condense
6. erected, built, raised, crated
7. furtive, secret, sly, evil
8. stingy, miserly, wealthy, grudging
9. caricature, character, parody, cartoon
10. reckless, rash, forbidden, wild

Choose the best word for each sentence.

1. Our community is educationally (onward, progressive, forward).
2. The attack was successfully (stopped, ended, repulsed).
3. We felt that the reward given the boy was (not enough, not sufficient, inadequate).
4. The law demanded that a (reward, remuneration, compensation) be given her for the loss.
5. The doctor said I had all the (symbols, marks, symptoms) of pneumonia.
6. A period of quiet thought is (solitude, consideration, meditation).
7. Recollections are (offerings, memories, reminders).
8. A person's distinguishing qualities make up his (inheritance, pride, character).
9. To be accompanied is to be (escorted, paid back, hired out).
10. A decree is an (honor, edict, invocation).

Similarities

A **synonym** is a word that has the same or nearly the same meaning as another word. But there are fine differences between synonyms that make one word more suitable than another.

Synonyms

The italicized words in the following sentences are synonyms for *take*. In which sentences is the synonym a better choice than *take*? In which are the two about even in effectiveness?

1. The hunters (took, *captured*) the bird.
2. Jim (took, *captured*) the trick with his ace.
3. Mary (took, *caught*) Eliza's hand.
4. The soldiers (took, *guzzled*) the water brought them.
5. He (took, *bought*) the first suit he saw.
6. The president (took, *adopted*) the chair.
7. It was time to (take, *choose*).
8. The sailor (took, *employed*) a mop to the deck.
9. She (takes, *requires*) a size 38.

Below is a list of badly overworked general words. Copy them and write next to each several more specific words.

1. **look:** *glance, peer, stare, ogle, spy, squint, spot, view*
2. walk
3. see
4. seems
5. run
6. make
7. have
8. go
9. moved
10. funny
11. is/was
12. said
13. various
14. Cute
15. pretty
16. sweet
17. nice
18. beautiful
19. fine

Match the synonyms.

A	B	A	B
placidly	tasteless	fortitude	obstinate
stolid	agreeable	peaceful	sudden
reluctantly	spoiled	stubborn	prohibit
rancid	bear	forbid	serene
endure	unexcitable	exuberant	hint
sullenly	peacefully	abrupt	joyful
amicable	forcefulness	fragrance	annoying
vehemence	ill-humoredly	irksome	scent
bland	unwillingly	inkling	strength

Antonyms

Use at least five of these words to describe someone you know. Check a dictionary for meanings you are unsure of.

capricious	magnanimous
diffident	neurotic
garrulous	obtuse
hypocritical	officious
indefatigable	reticent
insipid	stolid
jocular	taciturn

Experimenting with *antonyms* is another good way to build your vocabulary. Match the columns for opposite meanings.

A	B	A	B
abhor	contempt	nice	nadir
barbarism	obscure	to ornament	worker
cause	prevent	truce	plain
cheap	culture	quiet	attack
esteem	detach	recent	heavenly
famous	gentle	shelter	agitated
grimy	express	terrestrial	deface
harsh	love	unfathomable	crude
imply	spotless	vagabond	dissension
join	boldness	withdrawal	surrender
keep	forego	yield	introduction
learning	ignorance	zenith	intelligible
modesty	costly	variegated	ancient

Write the antonym of the first italicized word. Then change the second word in italics to show how the antonym changes the meaning.

1. The *complexity* of the problem made it *difficult* to explain.
2. Her *disparaging* remark *humiliated* me.
3. Because my client is wholly *innocent* of the crime, he should be *acquitted*.
4. The *fresh* air in the corridor *revived* me.

5. Because of his *implacable* decisions, the leader was *detested*.
6. An *arrogant* manner invites *rebellion*.
7. His *narrow* mental horizons were reflected in his *petty* spirit.
8. Anita's *artificial* concern for others drew only *frigid* responses.
9. Her *flushed* face revealed her *glowing* health.
10. The dancer's *willowy* movements reminded me of *gossamer*.

No one has to tell you that a product called Corn-o-cide is intended to get rid of corns. You recognize that the form *-cide* means "the killing of someone or something"; *suicide*, for example, means killing one's self.

FEET HURT?
WASH AWAY CORNS, CALLOUSES & PAIN
WITH
Corn-O-Cide®

FOOT SPECIALIST'S EXCLUSIVE FORMULA!
FASTEST, SAFEST WAY TO REMOVE CORNS & CALLOUSES.

There are many other English word parts that you can learn to identify quickly. Knowing them can help you build a stronger vocabulary. The word *transportation*, for instance, has three parts, and each part has a meaning.

Prefix	Root	Suffix
trans-	port	-ation
"across"	"carry"	"the action of"

Even if you had never heard the word *transportation* before, as long as you knew the parts, you would get the idea that it means "a carrying across."

The root of a word is its main part, the source of its meaning. Some words go back to the Latin. Others go back farther, to the Greek. Even the everyday words you use have a connection with ancient languages. These words that name the parts of human body were used in the days of Roman chariots. They are the source of some words today.

pedis	Latin, "foot"	*pedal*	"lever operated by foot"
manus	Latin, "hand"	*manicure*	"care of the hands"
dens, dentis	Latin, "tooth"	*dental*	"pertaining to teeth"
oculus	Latin, "eye"	*oculist*	"an eye doctor"

By studying the roots of these words, you may be able to discover their meaning. Match the two columns.

pedestrian	writing done by hand
manuscript	one who walks
dentifrice	a hundred-footed insect
monocle	a doctor who straightens teeth
centipede	an eye glass for one eye
orthodontist	a cleaning agent for teeth
manual	a "handy" book, one that can easily be handled

Word Roots   7

Choosing from the words listed, fill in the blanks.

   dentist   manual   oculist   pedestrian   podiatrist

After receiving a clean bill of health from the (foot doctor) ____, the (eye doctor) ____ and (the doctor who examined his teeth) ____, the ____ was killed crossing the street because he failed to read the (handy guide book) ____ saying that cars can now turn right on red.

You've probably already noticed that roots may change slightly. Over so many years, you'd almost expect that. Sometimes the changes are in the last letter or two as in the root *aster* which means "star." It forms the word *asteroid*, "little star," but it also is the base for *astrodome*, a room through which you can see the stars. Sometimes the changes are within the root. A *tripod* is a three-footed stand. Its root *ped* changes to *pod*. Don't be put off by these minor changes. If the essential features were there, you wouldn't mistake a friend just because of a suntan or a new hairdo. Which other roots changed slightly?

These roots describe earth and sky.

aqua	"water"	aquarium:	a glass tank holding water animals and plants
aster, astro	"star"	asteroid:	little star
geo	"earth"	geography:	science of picturing earth
luna	"moon"	lunar:	pertaining to the moon
sol	"sun"	solar:	pertaining to the sun
terr	"land"	terrarium:	a bowl containing earth and plants
urb	"city"	urban:	pertaining to city

Study the roots and match the meanings.

   suburb   a science that measures the earth
   territory   a subdivision of a city
   geometry   someone who goes mad at full moon

8   Word Roots

aquaplane — one who travels in the space between the stars
lunatic — a definite area of land
solarium — a plane that can land on water
astronaut — a room with many windows to let the sun in

Using the words listed, fill the blanks.

aquatic   "growing or living in water"

aqueduct   "pipe for carrying water"

disaster   "unfavorable aspect of the stars, tragedy"

suburban   "areas outside the city"

terrestrial   "belonging to earth"

urban   "within the city"

_____ animals are of great variety and beauty. One of the biggest _____ of our age is that lake and stream pollution are killing off many species of fish. _____ renewal only adds to the waste that must be discharged into the water systems running into the seas. The Romans used _____ as moderns use sewers, but their population was smaller. As a result of so much waste, not only fish but human beings can't find pure water, even in the outskirts of the city — the _____. The whole of _____ existence seems in danger of extinction.

How many of these do you know the word for? The italicized word suggests the root.

1. A system of the universe with the *sun* as center.
2. A famous sea in mid-Europe surrounded by *land*.
3. A flower with petals arranged like a *star*.
4. A color like *seawater*.
5. One who makes predictions about the fortunes of people by studying the *stars*.
6. A word describing something below the *land*.
7. The study of the history of the *earth*.

Word Roots

Study these Latin roots and the words derived from them.

annus	"a year"	*biannual:* twice a year
audio	"to hear"	*audience:* a group who hears
brevis	"short"	*brevity:* shortness
caput	"the head"	*cap:* head covering
forma	"a form, a shape"	*inform:* give knowledge a form
finis	"the end, a limit"	*definite:* set to a limit
lex, legis	"a law"	*legitimate:* lawful
liber	"a book"	*liberty:* freedom because of education by books
locus	"a place"	*locality:* a particular place
magnus	"great"	*magnificent:* something great
bellum	"war"	*antebellum:* before the war
centum	"a hundred"	*centenary:* a hundred-year anniversary

Find the same roots in these twelve words, then decide which word fits each sentence.

decapitate	belligerent	abbreviate	magnify
century	finish	auditorium	formulate
local	annual	legal	library

1. The guillotine was used to ____ the rebels.
2. I wish the committee would ____ their plans on paper.
3. The minister should ____ his sermons on hot Sundays.
4. The ____ fair always draws a crowd of ten thousand.
5. My grandfather, age 96, is almost a ____ old.
6. When you ____ cleaning the garage, you can start on the cellar.
7. The ____ held over a thousand people.

8. Our neighborhood ____ has 100,000 books.
9. This laser microscope can ____ things millions of times.
10. His ____ attitude gets him into many fights.
11. The ____ bus system costs a quarter a ride.
12. Besides court costs, ____ counsel will come to $500.

Write your own sentence using each word.

Study each root individually, and match each word to its definition.

cyclus   "circle, wheel"   *bicycle:* two-wheeler

recycle	one wheel
cyclic	to use again and again
unicycle	one who rides a bicycle
cyclone	moving in circles
cyclist	a storm characterized by circular winds
cyclatron	a machine for directing atoms to be smashed in spiral fashion
tricycle	three-wheeler

vocare   "to call"   *vocation:* a calling

invoke	to call on
revoke	without spoken sound
provoke	spoken sounds
vocal	to call back again
avocation	one who sings
vocabulary	human organ of speaking
vocalist	words known
voice	to call forth or arouse
voiceless	hobby, not one's calling

Word Roots

dicere "to speak" *dictionary:* a book of words

diction	to say ahead of time
dictaphone	to formally accuse
dictate	word choice
dictator	a machine for conveying the sound of words
dictum	to speak for someone to write down
indict	one who commands by his words
predict	one who says "yes" again and again to a habit
addict	a formal statement

Although it is spelled the same, the pronunciation of this word is quite different from the others: \in-'dīt\.

mortis "death" *mortuary:* a temporary place for the dead

mortician	subject to death
post mortem	a payment "killed off" in small amounts
mortal	not ever dying
immortal	examination after death
mortify	to cause shame or humiliation: little deaths
mortgage	undertaker

vita "life" *vital:* important to life

vitamin	to give life
vitality	an element in food that was thought to contain substances essential to life
vitalize	state of being full of life
revitalize	to put life into again

venire "to come" *convention:* a coming together of many people

convene	growing out of standards accepted by large numbers of persons

Word Roots

conventional   a house where nuns come together to live religious lives

convent   to come together

adventure   easy to come to, do or use

convenient   a coming to things that involve risk

Combine the following word forms with the root *logy* to form the names of the sciences that are defined.

logos   "word, science, study of"   *mythology:* the science or study of myths

archaeo-	ancient, old
astro-	star
bio-	life
cyto-	cells
embryo-	fetus
etymo-	literal sense of a word
geo-	earth
grapho-	picture making, drawing
neuro-	nerves
physio-	laws of nature
psyche-	spirit, mind
theo-	god

Definitions
1. the study of cells
2. the study of the earth's crust
3. the study of living things
4. the study of the stars
5. the study of embryonic life
6. the study of ancient cultures by excavation

Word Roots 13

7. the study of handwriting
8. the study of the origin and development of words
9. the study of the nervous system
10. the study of religion
11. the study of physical processes
12. the study of the mind

How many words can you make with the subjects you formed above by using this suffix: *-ist* which means "one who does"? Example: *neurologist* **"a doctor who treats diseases of the nervous system."**

Using these words, fill in the blanks.

addicted	psychology
adventurous	vital
cycle	vitality
immortality	vocalist
mortal	voice
mortified	

    Judy Garland was a (singer) ____ who *performed* during the rainbow era of showbiz. Only four-foot-eleven, she was always (figuratively, made to die) ____ by her stocky body, but her *magnificently* (lively) ____ (larynx) ____ brought her (undying fame) ____ in the show world. Some say she became (saying "yes" again and again to a habit) ____ to the drugs she was forced to take to keep to movie production schedules, but a recent *biographer* said that the tragedy of her life proceeded partly from an unusually (coming out to new experiences involving risk) ____ imagination. It set up ideals that she could not reconcile with her merely (dying) ____ circumstances. Although her inner (study of the mind) ____ was one (circle) ____ of disappointments after another, the image she still projects is one of *infinite* (liveliness) ____.

Drawing from all the roots you've studied so far, can you tell what the italicized words in the paragraph mean?

Word Roots

Here are ten more roots for study. When you are familiar with them, stretch your understanding by filling in the blanks in the sentences with related words from the list.

duc, duct	"to lead"	*to conduct*: to lead or direct
fer	"to bear, carry"	*to defer*: to put off carrying, postpone
ject	"to throw"	*projection*: something thrown forward
mis, mit	"to send"	*to transmit*: to send across
pen, pend	"to hang"	*depend*: to hang on, to lean on
port	"to carry"	*portable*: capable of being carried
pos	"to place"	*position*: a place
rupt	"to break"	*disrupt*: to break up
script	"to write"	*manuscript*: something written by hand
spir	"to breathe, give life"	*spirit*: that which gives life

appendix	injection	remittance
conference	inspire	ruptured
deposit	missionary	scripture
ductless	offering	spirited
induce	rejected	transport

1. They rushed him to the hospital for a _____ appendix.
2. The men carried on a dialogue about the new jetport at a _____ that lasted three hours.
3. What did you say to _____ him to write so lovely a poem?
4. The rally was full of life, very _____.
5. A _____ dryer, because it does not allow the lint and moisture to escape, produces a dusty house.

6. The ____ carried his religion to foreign lands.
7. You can find additional material at the end of the book, the ____.
8. Can you ____ Wendy to come with us on the trip?
9. Mort is deflated because he was ____ for the choir.
10. The Sacred ____ were written over a period of 1500 years.
11. How much money did you ____ in the bank last week?
12. Send your ____ by check or money order to the New York office.
13. What ____ will you make in the collection basket?
14. They gave her an ____ in the arm.
15. The ____ company hauls thousands of tons of merchandise annually.

PREFIXES COME FIRST

A **prefix** is a word part that comes before the root, or base word, and changes its meaning in some way. The easiest prefixes to learn are associated with numbers. You probably know most of them.

mono	one	**tri**	three	**hex**	six
uni	one	**quad**	four	**sex**	six
duo	two	**pent**	five	**sept**	seven
di	two	**quin**	five	**oct**	eight
bi	two			**nona**	nine
				dec	ten

How many?

bi-monthly ____ a month
tripod ____ legs
octagonal ____ sided
nonagenarian ____ years old
decimal numbered by ____'s

Prefixes

septennial   ___ years
pentagon   ___ sided figure
duet   ___ voices performing
monogamy   marriage to ___ persons
quintet   ___ in the group
unilateral   ___ sided
quadrangle   ___ angles

Match these:

every three months	octagon
six-sided	decibel
70 years old	tri-monthly
every two years	hexagonal
eight-sided figure	unicycle
three voices	trio
one ruler	monarch
five children born together	biennial
one-wheeled vehicle	quintuplets
sound measure based on multiples of ten	septuagenarian

Tell the number associated with each of these and the meaning of the word if you know it.

monosyllabic	bicycle
monogram	biplane
monologue	triangle
monotonous	triplets
uniform	trinity
unison	quintet
unite	sextuplets
bifocals	octogenarian
duet	octopus
biped	December

Handy Prefixes to Know

    pre-   "before"   *premature*: before ripe

    post-   "after"   *postdate*: to date after the date of writing

Match each definition with the right word.

1. To think about beforetime, as a murder   prefabricate
2. A word part that goes before a word   postscript
3. Sentences added after the signature of a letter   premonition
4. To go before, as in a line   postpone
5. Make up beforehand for easy assembling   postgraduate
6. A student who studies after graduating with a degree   precede
7. An inkling of something before it happens   prefix
8. To put off until a later time   premeditate

    sub-   "under"   *subway*: a passageway underground

    super-   "above, on, over"   *superman*: someone with above-human powers

Match each definition with the right word.

1. underwater   submit
2. below the conscious level   subculture
3. to plunge under water   superimpose
4. to give in to someone over you   superhighway
5. above the speed of sound   supersonic
6. a culture developed within another culture   subconscious
7. a broad road for high speed traffic   submarine
8. to impose over   submerge

trans- "across" *transmitter:* an instrument for sending messages across distances

circum- "around" *circumference:* The distance around a circle

Match each definition with the right word.

1. across the Atlantic — circumnavigate
2. to cross over or change, as from vehicle to vehicle — circumspect
3. to sail completely around the world — translate
4. talking in circles — transact
5. looking around, being careful — transfer
6. to carry across a business deal — circumlocution
7. to change across languages — transatlantic
8. having a direct object because the verb passes the action across from the subject — transitive

Tell what the following words mean.

1. suburban
2. supernatural
3. transcribe
4. circumvent
5. preview

anti- "against" *antidote:* a remedy against poison

ante- "before" *anteroom:* a room before some other room

Match each definition with the right word.

1. Before the war (bellum = "war" in Latin) — antedate
2. to predate — antibiotic
3. a substance used to fight against harmful micro-organisms — antecedent
4. a word that means the opposite of another word — anti-busing
5. a word that comes before a pronoun — antiseptic

6. a substance that fights against the growth of bacteria — antipathy
7. against the busing issue — antonym
8. a feeling of dislike for another — antebellum

inter- "between" *international*: between countries

intra-, intro- "into, within" *intramural*: within the walls of one school

Match each definition with the right word.

1. to break into, especially in speech — introvert
2. a time between, as between acts of a play — interrupt
3. one who turns inward — intersect
4. given into the veins — introduce
5. to stop progress, as to get the other team's ball — intercept
6. to bring in for the first time — intercede
7. to go between and plead for — intravenous
8. to meet and to cut through at a point — intermission

mal- "bad" *malnutrition*: poor eating habits

bene- "well" *benefit*: something done for the good of another

Match each definition with the right word.

1. spiteful — malignant
2. one who receives good things, as in a will — benediction
3. failure in professional skill that leads to harm — malicious
4. producing death, as a tumor — malpractice
5. a blessing — benefactor
6. an abnormal shape — beneficial
7. describing something good for you — malformation
8. someone who does evil to another — malefactor

Match either of these prefixes with the words below. Tell what each finished word means. If you aren't sure, check your dictionary.

semi- "half"		mis- "wrong"
pronounce	deal	step
inform	fit	annual
circle	spell	trust
calculate	conscious	fire

Choose the right word for each blank.

benevolence, maltreated, predated, international, antipathy,

malicious, introspection, misinformed, semiannual

1. He ____ the check three days before the deadlines.
2. The child was not ____, only mischievous.
3. It was an ____ conference, not merely local.
4. They didn't get along because of her ____ for him.
5. She wasn't outgoing but rather given to ____.
6. Mrs. Grim's ____ to birds brought them to her yard in droves.
7. At the ____ meeting, the corporation reviewed its profits.
8. We must have been ____ about the time.

Common Prefixes

prefix	means	as in
ab-	"from, away"	*absent*
ad- (ac-, af-, al-, ap-, as-, at-)	"to, toward" (spelling changes according to following letter)	*admit* *acquire, affect,* *attract*
auto-	"self"	*autobiography*
co- (com-, col-, con-)	"with, together" (spelling changes)	*cosign* *commit, collect*

Prefixes

contra-	"against"	*contradict*
de-	"from, down"	*deflate*
dis-	"the opposite of"	*disagree*
ex-	"out, from"	*exclude*
in- (il-, im-, ir)	"not" (spelling changes)	*inactice* *illogical, irregular*
per-	"through, by means of"	*percolate*
pro-	"before"	*program*
re-	"again"	*relocate*
un-	"not"	*unusual*

Briefly tell the difference in meaning between the words in each set.

1. invert, revert
2. discredit, accredit
3. admission, intermission
4. monologue, dialogue
5. transform, deform
6. malefactor, benefactor
7. receive, deceive
8. depreciate, appreciate
9. impulse, repulse
10. provide, divide

Use each of the following words in a sentence.

1. abnormal
2. anteroom
3. disconnect
4. project
5. illegitimate
6. circumnavigate
7. antibody
8. postmortem
9. miscalculate
10. immature

The Latest Thing

Popular songs have taken many themes over the years. This early American song was a toast to George Washington. Notice that the letter "s" is printed two ways. When is it in the form we know today? Can you deduce the meaning of a "bumper"?

Brother Soldiers all hail!

A Favorite New Patriotic Song In Honor of Washington.

"Heaven has lent him in love to mankind"

To which is added

A TOAST Written & Composed by F. Hopkinson, Esqr.

Price 37 Cents

Printed and fold at B Carr's Mufical Repofitory Philadelphia J Carr's Baltimore & J Hewitt's N York

'Tis WASHINGTONS Health fill a bumper all round for he is our glory and pride our arms fhall in battle with conqueft be crown'd whilft virtue and he's on our fide our arms fhall in battle with conqueft be crown'd whilft virtue and he's on our fide and he's on our fide

2
'Tis WASHINGTONS Health loud cannons fhould roar,
And trumpets the truth fhood proclaim
There cannot be found fearch all the world o'er
His equal in virtue and fame

3
'Tis WASHINGTONS Health our Hero to blefs
May heaven look gracioufly down
Oh long may he live our hearts to poffefs
And freedom ftill call him her own

SUFFIXATION

The word *suffixation* is a good example of what the word means. A suffix is a group of letters added to the end of a word or root that changes the meaning—and usually the function—of the word. The suffix *-ation* means "the act of something"; therefore, suffixation is the act of adding a suffix.

Some suffixes are immediately familiar; you recognize and use them without really needing to identify their meaning. The following suffixes fall into that category. They change a noun or adjective into a verb.

suffix	means	as in
-ate	"act on or cause to be changed"	*activate, generate*
-en	"cause to be or have"	*strengthen, deepen*
-fy, -ify	"make"	*beautify, deify*
-ize	"cause to resemble"	*sterilize, familiarize*

Add one of the verb-forming suffixes to each root or word listed and write a sentence with the new word. If you are not sure you have the right combination, check the dictionary. Watch for spelling changes.

ample, light, motive, memory, glory, natural, caliber, simple, sharp, mobile, critic

Another group of suffixes are those that form adjectives.

suffix	means	as in
-able, -ible	"able to"	*capable, legible*
-al	"pertaining to"	*musical, legal*
-ary	"pertaining to"	*elementary, library*
-ed	"resembling; like"	*conceited, ragged*
-ful	"full of"	*joyful, graceful*

-ic	"derived from; pertaining to"	*alcoholic, electronic*
-ish	"like; somewhat"	*childish, yellowish*
-less	"without"	*colorless, countless*
-ous, -eous, -ious	"full of"	*adventurous, courageous, ambitious*
-y	"resembling, possessing"	*cloudy, shiny*

Use the following words and the adjective-forming suffixes to make a list of adjectives. Then choose a suitable adjective for each sentence.

accident, blood, allergy, water, motion, right, second, book, nostalgia, plenty, spirit, convert, athlete, depend, malice

1. You can sleep on the _____ sofa tonight.
2. His _____ slip of the tongue embarrassed everyone.
3. The _____ horse was impossible to control.
4. There is a _____ supply of hot dogs.
5. That clock is not very _____.
6. The calm sea was deceptively _____.
7. She had an _____ reaction to the serum.
8. This soup is so _____ it has no taste.
9. His air of _____ indignation turned us off.
10. She gets very _____ about the fifties.
11. A _____ child, he was always reading.
12. What a mess! The baby has a _____ nose!
13. He has won an _____ scholarship because of his football record.
14. That _____ child has broken the swing!
15. Your problems are of _____ concern to those of the whole group.

MUGGEE

Here's an odd-looking, unfamiliar word that you won't find in the dictionary. But you can figure out its meaning if you think of its counterpart: *mugger*.

The difference in meaning between such word pairs as *employer* and *employee* points up the importance of suffixes. The largest group of suffixes are those that form nouns. The following suffixes attach to verbs or to other nouns to add the meaning "one who does something," "one who lives in a place" or, in the case of *-ee*, "one who receives something."

suffix	as in
-ant	*participant*
-ee	*grantee*
-eer	*pamphleteer*
-er	*reporter, New Yorker*
-ian	*Martian*
-ist	*cyclist, socialist*
-ite	*Brooklynite*

Another group of suffixes conveys the meaning of "an action or process" of doing something.

suffix	as in
-al	*rehearsal*
-ance	*performance*
-ation	*flirtation*
-ence	*emergence*
-ism	*criticism*
-ment	*development*

Some of the suffixes in the second group have an additional meaning, "the state or quality" of something. Suffixes with this meaning include:

suffix	as in
-age	*dotage*
-ation	*starvation*
-cy	*idiocy*
-dom	*freedom*
-ence	*reference*
-ery	*slavery*
-hood	*motherhood*
-ity	*theatricality*
-ness	*goodness*
-ship	*friendship*

Add one (or more, if you can) of the noun-forming suffixes to each of these roots. Then write a sentence with each new word.

perspire	resist	same
dictate	judge	sane
announce	optometry	teach
accept	drama	agreeable
commit	inspire	salty
ignore	memorize	accurate

Because English is a versatile language, many words are formed not only from prefixes, suffixes and roots but also from parts of words called *combining forms*. You have already met one.

Combining Forms

Take another look at page 5.

    -cide "killing" *insecticide:* a substance that kills insects

Combine these base forms with the combining form *-cide* into new words. Then match the definitions.

pater-	"father"	**homi-**	"man"
mater-	"mother"	**germi-**	"germ"
soror-	"sister"	**pesti-**	"bothersome insect"
frater-	"brother"	**geno-**	"a whole group of people"
sui-	"self"	**regi-**	"king"

1. taking one's own life
2. manslaughter
3. killing of a father
4. killing of a king
5. killing of a sister
6. killing of a mother
7. killing of a nation
8. killing of a brother
9. killing of bothersome bugs
10. killing of germs

    -archy "rule" *autarchy:* rule by oneself

Combine the following base forms, or others, with the combining form *-archy*, then match the definitions.

    an- without, not   **mon-** one   **olig-** a few

1. rule by one king
2. rule by a small group
3. rule by a father
4. confusion, no rule

    -graph, -gram "written picture; capable of writing or drawing" *geography:* picture or map of the earth

Make the combinations and match the final words to the correct definitions.

tele-	"distant"	**crypto-**	"hidden"
typo-	"type"	**mono-**	"one"

1. pertaining to type
2. a message sent from afar
3. a single design giving initials
4. message in code

-poly- "many" *polyphony*: many sounds

tele- "from a distance" *telegraph*: signals from afar

How many roots in this list include the adjective-forming suffix *-ic*?

Match either combining form that fits with the roots below. Then give the correct word for each definition.

-glot	"tongue"
-scope	"instrument for seeing"
-pathy	"feeling, communication"
-photo	"light"
-gamy	"marriage"
-syllabic	"syllable"
-technic	"practical arts"
-cast	"broadcast"
-vision	"sight"
-theism	"belief in god"
-phone	"instrument for sound"
-gon	"sided figure"
-chromatic	"characteristic of color"
-valent	"values"
-nomial	"name of terms"

1. broadcast from a long way off
2. many marriages at one time
3. belief in many gods
4. many-sided figures
5. having many syllables
6. one who speaks many languages

7. communication between minds
8. instrument for viewing things far away
9. many sounds
10. composed of many colors

Write either the definition or a sentence for each of the words not defined above.

  micro- "small, minute" *microprint:* small print

  macro- "long, large" *macroscopic:* large enough to be seen by naked eye

  auto- "self" *automobile:* vehicle driven by oneself

  -tomy "cut" *tonsillectomy:* cutting out of tonsils

If you add *micro-* to these base words, what do you get?

  -biology "study of living things"

  -print "reproduce by pressing an inked form"

  -scope "machine for seeing"

  -wave "undulation that transfers energy"

If you add *macro-* to these base words, what do you get?

  -cyte "cell"

  -evolution "change"

  -scale "measuring device"

If you add *auto-* to these base words, what do you get?

  -biography "story of a life"

  -hypnosis "sleep-producing"

  -graph "something written"

  -matic "done spontaneously and unconsciously"

Combining Forms

Tell the difference between these sets.

psychic, psychosomatic	solar, lunar
telescope, microscope	ocular, dental
polygamy, monogamy	astrology, geology
macrocosm, microcosm	aquatic, terrestrial
automatic, manual	unicycle, tricycle
polysyllabic, monosyllabic	convene, disrupt
appendectomy, tonsillectomy	reject, project
psychology, psychiatry	cyclist, pedestrian
monotheism, polytheism	deduction, induction
pedicure, manicure	scriptography, typography

Using as many of the combining forms as you can, create the story suggested by this picture.

More, More

Now that you are familiar with combining forms, they should come more easily. Study the meaning of these common ones and work the exercises below each set.

arch-	"chief, great"	*archrival:* main foe
biblio-	"book"	*bibliophile:* lover of books
bio-	"life"	*biology:* study of living things
contra-	"against"	*contramand:* command against given orders
-cracy	"government"	*democracy:* government of the people
endo-	"within"	*endoskeleton:* bones within the skin
exo-	"out of"	*exogamy:* outside marriage
hetero-	"different"	*heterogeneous:* originating from different bodies
homo-	"same"	*homonym:* words sounding the same
hydro-	"water"	*hydroelectric:* energy from water

Match these.

1. story of one's own life
2. clash of opinions
3. government of the people
4. mixed the same throughout
5. grafted from another species
6. seaplane
7. chief foe
8. holy book
9. inner lining
10. far out

bible
endoderm
heterograft
autobiography
democracy
homogenized
controversy
exotic
archenemy
hydroplane

Combining Forms

Complete these statements.

1. Because the lobster has an *exoskeleton*, it is necessary to (crack its outer shell, pick out the bones).
2. *Homogenized* milk has the cream (mixed throughout, on top).
3. A *heterogeneous* class is one in which students are (tracked by ability, all mixed together within the group).
4. The *endocrine* glands secrete hormones (into the bloodstream, outside the blood system).
5. (Water, Air) is the healer in *hydrotherapy*.
6. A *biography* is the written story of (a life, a death).
7. He needed three more (books, bibles) to complete his *bibliography*.
8. In Abdullah Hallal's *autocracy*, (Abdullah Hallal himself, a group of rulers) reigned supreme.
9. When the police discovered the *contraband* the men were sent to (prison, Washington for honors).

-meter	"measure"	*barometer*: instrument for measuring atmospheric pressure
omni-	"all"	*omnivorous*: eating everything, both meat and vegetables
-onym	"name"	*synonym*: word with the same meaning
ortho-	"straight"	*orthodontist*: doctor who straightens teeth
pan-	"all, complete"	*panacea*: cure-all
philo-(e)	"loving"	*philosopher*: lover of wisdom
-phobe	"fear"	*claustrophobia*: fear of closed places
pseudo-	"false"	*pseudonym*: a fictitious name

Complete these statements.

1. Anglophiles, Francophiles and Sinophiles are (lovers, haters) of England, France and China respectively.

2. Chronometers, photometers and speedometers (measure, count) time, light and speed.

3. A photostatic copy is produced by means of (light rays, radio waves).

4. The phonograph, telephone and microphone are recent inventions for (sound, sight) transmission.

5. The omnipresent poverty (boosted, reduced) the morale of the citizens.

6. A heretic's opinions are (orthodox, unorthodox).

7. The panoramic view took in (the whole view, a certain, small view in detail).

8. Acrophobia and monophobia are (love of, fear of) high places and being alone.

9. Some people regard the study of UFO's and ESP as pseudo-sciences because the facts on which they are founded are (provable, unprovable).

Review: Tell the difference between the words in each pair.

confer, defer	aqueduct, viaduct
eject, reject	geography, astrology
append, depend	predict, dictate
erupt, corrupt	repose, transpose
pedal, manual	inspect, expect
dental, ocular	contract, retract
intercede, supercede	lustrous, translucent
aquarium, terrarium	precede, succeed
omit, remit	export, import
astronaut, aquanaut	inspire, expire

How many words can you make up using these as roots? Use the picture for ideas.

aqua-(water), **geo-**(earth), **script-**(write), **astro-**(star)

Review: What is the meaning of the root in each set of words?

1. bankrupt, erupt, rupture, disrupt, corrupt
2. zoology, biology, theology, astrology, chronology
3. vocation, invoke, revoke, vocal, provoke
4. reject, project, inject, conjecture, dejection
5. postscript, scripture, manuscript, inscribe, describe
6. spirit, inspire, perspire, respiration, conspire
7. conduct, deduct, induct, induce, produce
8. transportation, reporter, deport, porter, export
9. position, deposit, repose, depose, compose
10. pending, depend, appendage, appendix, compendium

RESOURCES

Language is alive and well and living and changing. Your language — English — is one of the most hospitable languages of all — ready to accept new words all the time. Are you keeping up? How many of these recently coined words do you know?

flextime	Aunt Tom	comparative advertising
ecocide	pull date	Jesus freak
water bed	alimony drone	love pollution

Ordinarily you'd refer to a dictionary to find the meaning of new words, but if your dictionary isn't hot off the press, you won't find some of the words on this list.

A good up-to-date dictionary is a valuable asset to your writing. You should know already that a dictionary provides all these items of information about words.

> correct and variant spelling
>
> word division, structure and abbreviations
>
> preferred and secondary pronunciations
>
> parts of speech
>
> word inflections and usage pointers
>
> mechanics: capitalization, underlining, hyphenation, spelling variations
>
> word origin and history
>
> meanings, including synonyms and sometimes antonyms

Which of the items in the list are given in your dictionary for these words?

> disposition   pensive   territory   kerb
> hero   posthumous   silhouette   aesthetic

Even with a dictionary at hand, pronounciation can be a bugbear unless you know how to interpret the pronunciation key at the bottom of the page. What is the pronunciation in most frequent usage for each of these words? You may have to check the guide at the beginning of the dictionary to discover how pronunciation variants are entered.

> Is **ch**asm sounded like **ch**ain or **c**ake?
>
> im**p**ious sounded like **pea** or **pie**?
>
> **coup**on sounded like **coo** or **cup**ie?
>
> **al**mond sounded like **all** or **ah**?

apricot sounded like **a**pe or **a**pple?

pal**m** sounded like **T**om or **a**l**ms**?

griev**ous** sounded like **us** or dev**ious**?

p**os**thumous sounded like h**ost** or **ost**eopath?

Where is the primary stress in each of these words?

imPOtent or IMpotent?   rePUTable or REPutable?

INfamous or inFAMous?   preFERable or PREFerable?

suPERfluous or superFLUous?   veHEment or VEHement?

MISchievous or misCHIEvous?   EXquisite or exQUIsite?

inCOMparable or incomPARable?   inCONgruous or inconGRUous?

Some words have several meanings. The first may not answer your need. How many different meanings does this word have?

¹**lid** \'lid\ *n* [ME, fr. OE *hlid;* akin to OHG *hlit* cover, OE *hlinian* to lean — more at LEAN] **1 :** a movable cover for the opening of a hollow container (as a vessel or box) **2 :** EYELID **3 :** the operculum in mosses **4** *slang* : HAT **5 :** RESTRAINT, CURB <put a ~ on further release of information> **6 :** an ounce of marijuana
²**lid** *vt* **lid·ded; lid·ding :** to cover or supply with a lid

Which meaning would fit these sentences? Answer by giving first the number of the entry and then the number and letter of the sub-entry.

1. Where'd you get that classy *lid*?
2. The committee put a *lid* on their operations.
3. The *lid* of that crate is loose.
4. Her *lids* were covered with a ghastly green paste.
5. Would you help *lid* these jelly jars?

By permission. From Webster's New Collegiate Dictionary © 1975 by G. & C. Merriam Co., Publishers of the Merriam-Webster Dictionaries.

Dictionary Skills

> ¹lick \'lik\ vb [ME *licken,* fr. OE *liccian;* akin to OHG *leckōn* to lick, L *lingere,* Gk *leichein*] vt **1 a** (1) : to draw the tongue over <~ a stamp> (2) : to flicker over like a tongue **b** : to take into the mouth with the tongue : LAP **2 a** : to strike repeatedly : THRASH **b** : to get the better of : OVERCOME <has ~ed every problem> ~ vi **1** : to lap with or as if with the tongue **2** : to dart like a tongue <flames ~ing out of windows> **3** : to move at top speed — **lick into shape** : to put into proper form or condition — **lick one's wounds** : to recover from injury
>
> ²lick *n* **1 a** : an act or instance of licking **b** : a small amount : BIT **c** : a hasty careless effort **2 a** : a sharp hit : BLOW **b** : OPPORTUNITY, TURN — usu. used in pl. **3** : a place (as a salt spring) to which animals regularly resort to lick a salt deposit **4** : a musical figure; *specif* : an interpolated and usu. improvised figure or flourish — **lick and a promise** : a perfunctory performance of a task

Which meaning would fit these sentences? Answer by giving first the number of the entry and then the number and letter of the sub-entry.

1. You won't *lick* that problem during this lab.
2. She gave her homework a *lick* and a promise.
3. In a *lick* the thief was gone.
4. The Panthers *licked* the Cougars last night.
5. He didn't care a *lick*.
6. The deer came regularly to the salt *lick*.
7. The flames *licked* the side of the barn.
8. Mr. Spratt *licked* his platter clean.
9. I want to get my *licks* in.
10. The little girl *licked* her cone expertly.

The dictionary explains idiomatic expressions at the end of the definition for the key word of the idiom. They are usually introduced by a dash and set in bold face. Find the meaning of the following idioms. In the first three, the word to consult is italicized. After that, you're on your own.

make *light* of	tie down	hold the line
to throw a *mean* curve	throw back	put upon
break up	all thumbs	look up
in kind	a far cry	farm out
over the hill	beat the rap	in a pig's eye
mixed bag	rat on	on the fly
shake-up (n.)	rule the roost	take after

Dictionary Skills 39

Picture That

Dictionaries also contain pictures, maps, tables, diagrams, graphs, and other pictorial information to clarify word meanings. Such illustrations are entered near the main word of the illustration. For instance, the table of measurements would be near the word *measure*. On what page in your dictionary do the following fall?

Morse code	diagram of a tooth
Braille alphabet	Signs of the Zodiac
Books of the Bible	Table of Roman Numerals
Table of Alphabets	Currency: Table of Exchange Rates

Tag Alongs

When you shop, you look at labels. What kinds of information can you find on them?

USE INSTEAD OF SOAP OR OTHER SKIN CLEANSERS

DIRECTIONS: After wetting the area to be scrubbed with warm water, squeeze out a 1-2 inch ribbon of Listerex on to hands and work into a lather with a small amount of water. Then gently massage Listerex into the skin with fingertips for about one minute. Rinse thoroughly with warm water and pat dry. Use once or twice daily.

CAUTION: Avoid contact with eyes. If contact with eyes occurs, rinse eyes thoroughly with water. If undue skin irritation develops, discontinue use and consult physician. For external use only. Keep this and all medication out of reach of children.

ACTIVE INGREDIENT: Thymol

INT. LADIES GARMENT • UNION MADE • ILGWU AFL-CIO • WORKERS UNION
Made in U.S.A.

Warning: The Surgeon General Has Determined That Cigarette Smoking is Dangerous to Your Health.

PURE WOOL

The Woolmark label is your assurance of quality-tested products made of the world's best...Pure Wool.

The dictionary is your supermarket for words. Most of its words and meanings have no label. Unlabeled entries mean the word is standard. That is, it is acceptable wherever you go throughout the United States. But some words are labeled to help you understand their special uses. The four most common kinds of labels are: **time:** how much the word is used today, **style:** in what social situation the word is most suitable, **region:** in what region of the world the given meaning is accepted and **field:** whether the word has a special meaning in a subject field, or activity.

Like people, word meanings grow old, change and even die. Two labels, *obsolete* and *archaic*, tell you that the meaning following them is no longer in use. You may come across obsolete or archaic words in reading older works, but you will do well not to use them in your own writing except for special effect.

Which meanings for the following words are considered obsolete — that is, dead, unused since 1775? Which are archaic — old-fashioned?

knowledge	turn	err	dome	dole
faculty	knave	fain	nature	blink

Most dictionaries are put together from samples taken of the way people actually use language. They do not show how language *should* be used so much as how it *is being* used. For this reason dictionaries include a wide range of vocabulary, from that spoken by uneducated people to that used by the most learned. Except for substandard, no level is better than any other. Each has its purpose and place. The good writer knows how to use each appropriately. You can discover the most common usage labels by looking up the following words.

rap (take the)	glitter	two bits
ain't	out (as of the question)	irregardless
(a) grind	pack (a pistol)	minus
slob	kisser	parallel

Dictionary Skills

Depending on which dictionary you consulted, you should have discovered these four or five usage lables.

substandard—considered unacceptable by educated persons

nonstandard—widely used but considered by the majority as unacceptable

colloquial—used in daily conversation and informal, personal writing but not polished enough for formal writing

informal—slightly more educated and polished colloquial usage but not always suitable for the most formal writing

slang—words, forceful, extravagant or witty figures of speech that are not standard or conventional, but may be appropriate in very informal situations for producing special effects

Language that is accepted by most people for most situations is considered *standard usage* and not labeled in the dictionary. Most words fall into this category.

What labels of style are connected with any of the definitions listed for the words below?

1. somewheres	1. blast	1. bozo
2. business	2. credent	2. drownded
3. egg	3. cut corners	3. hook
4. lulu	4. out	4. hit (the books)
5. ivory	5. knock off	5. malarkey
6. gray	6. grim	6. crackerjack
7. gray matter	7. hood	7. corker
8. mad (about)	8. lazy	8. hole up
9. roll up	9. salt	9. hob
10. guts	10. private eye	10. cool one's heels

Write a few sentences incorporating at least five of the words that were labeled *slang*. Keep the level of these sentences slang.

Write a standard paragraph that includes at least three of ten words that you found to be standard. Keep a somewhat formal tone throughout.

If you've ever traveled more than a few hundred miles, you've no doubt heard words used differently from the way you use them. What is a pancake to you may be a flapjack or a griddle cake to others. The dictionary labels that mark regional variations are as follows: **dial** for dialect: several regions hold the meaning.
N (North), **New Eng** (New England), **Midland, South, West, Southwest, Northwest**: peculiar to the region named
Scot (Scotland), **Brit** (Britain), **Canad** (Canada), **Irish, Austral** (Australia): standard in these English-speaking countries

In which regions are the following words used? Are the words standard or non-standard in these areas?

canuck	turn	petrol
bonny clabber	fall	acequia
syne	jaybird	himself
draught	lightwood	sundowner
cannikin	stonewall	knap
potlatch	mavourneen	larrup

Field labels tell the technical meaning of a word when used in a special subject field of knowledge or activity. These are the main field labels:

Astrology	Golf	Nautical
Baseball	Grammar	Philosophy
Card Games	Law	Politics
Chemistry	Linguistics	Printing
Commerce	Math	Sports
Drama	Medicine	Theology
Electrical	Music	Wrestling

Which meanings of the following words are restricted to use in a particular field? What field?

hit   form   pocket   leader   proof

Can You Top This?

A good dictionary carries much more information than just definitions. To answer the following questions, consult a collegiate or an unabridged dictionary. Not all dictionaries carry the same information; you may have to consult more than one.

1. **Abbreviations:** What do the following abbreviations stand for: DEW, PAYE, UNA?
2. **Arbitrary Signs and Symbols:** What do the following mean? ℞ λ
3. **Proofreader's Marks:** What do these indicate? ~~count~~ℓ Mr. Cent(re) queen
4. **Biographical Names:** Who were Vasco Nuñez de Balboa, Alma Gluck, Malcolm X (Malcolm Little)?
5. **A Pronouncing Gazeteer:** What and where are the Andes? the Pillars of Hercules? Timbuktu?
6. **Forms of Address:** What are the proper forms of address for the Attorney General, a mayor and a rabbi?
7. **Vocabulary of Rhymes:** What rhymes are listed for the sounds *arv*, *ort* and *ush*?
8. **Spelling:** How many spelling rules are listed? What is the difference between words ending in *or* and the same words ending in *our*? In the U.S., which is more widely used, the *ize* or the *ise* spelling?
9. **Plurals:** What is meant by the *zero plural?* (See animals.) Which word is pluralized in a three-word compound? Which six nouns change the middle vowel to form their plural?
10. **Punctuation:** What is a *virgule?* Under what three basic categories are commas treated? What is the second function of brackets?
11. **Compounds:** What is the last rule in the section about?
12. **Capitalization:** Which names of heavenly bodies should be capitalized? Which left in lower case?
13. **College and Universities:** Where is John Brown University? In what state is Oberlin College? When was Salem College, N.C., founded? Where is Bowdoin College?
14. **Miscellaneous:** Where is a dialect map shown in your dictionary? Is there a chart of Indo-European Languages? Where? What helps are given for writing a research paper? Is there a Table of Weights and Measures? What special articles does the dictionary contain at the front of the book?

KEYS TO RESEARCH

There is probably nothing more frustrating than wasting hours looking for a little piece of information that is absolutely essential to your paper. Learning to work the key references in the library can open up doors to better compositions in a minimum of time.

Card Catalogue

Everything in the library is indexed on 3 × 5 cards in a file known as the card catalogue. The file itself is alphabetical, but the items indexed are listed in one of two ways — by the Dewey Decimal system or the Library of Congress method. The Dewey Decimal system arranges books by numbers into ten classes based on ten main disciplines. Each hundred stands for one class. Books marked 100-199 are on philosophy. Books from 400-499 are on language. The Library of Congress uses letters of the alphabet to signal main fields of study. Numbers are used to subdivide the topics. The identifying letters and numbers of a book are the *call number*.

Which method does your library use? What are the call numbers of the following books?

1. A book on watercolor, aeronautics, photography
2. Any book by Carl Jung
3. The Bible
4. *The Bermuda Triangle*
5. *Harry S. Truman* by Margaret Truman

The card catalogue indexes books in three ways: by the author, by the subject and by the title.

1. Give the full title and name of the author of a book in your library about etiquette, one on botany and one on the F.B.I.
2. Give the call number and title of two books to be found under a topic of your own choice.
3. Name two books written by Pelham Grenville Wodehouse.
4. Who wrote *Frankenstein, The Thirteen Clocks, Don Juan?* When was each first published?
5. How many books does your library have by Mark Twain?

Encyclopedias

A book or set of books giving information on all or many branches of knowledge in alphabetically listed articles is an *encyclopedia*. You can find the subject or person you are looking for by referring directly to an entry or by searching out cross references labeled *See also* or *q.v.*, short for Latin *quod vide* which means "Which see." The best approach, however, is to find your subject in the index volume.

Consult an encyclopedia to answer these questions.

1. How did Death Valley get its name? What is the annual rainfall there?
2. What are some of the famous jewels in the imperial state crown of England?
3. What are some common North American butterflies?
4. Consult the index volume of any encyclopedia to find the titles of three articles on hunting dogs.
5. Some encyclopedias keep up on latest developments with a yearly supplement. What three articles of interest do you find in one of these volumes?

Almanacs and Yearbooks

You will find statistical information on world events in almanacs and yearbooks compiled yearly. Some of them are the *World Almanac*, *The New York Times Almanac*, *Information Please* and the *Statesman's Yearbook*.

Use one of them to answer these questions.

1. What was the longest baseball game in major league history?
2. Who won the Pulitzer prize for spot news photography last year?
3. How many people are killed by automobiles in the U.S. each year?
4. What boats were involved in the latest marine disaster? How many persons died?
5. What recordings won prizes in any year within the past three? What prizes were awarded?

6. What are the three highest mountains in the world, the five longest rivers and the three highest waterfalls?
7. How many telephones does New York City have?
8. Which state had the largest number of divorces in the latest recorded year? How many did it have?
9. Which country in the Middle East produces the largest amount of crude petroleum? How much does it produce? Which non-Middle East country produces the most? How much?
10. What is the official language of the Channel Islands? Where are they?

Atlases and Gazetteers

A dictionary or index of geographical names is a *gazetteer*. A bound edition of maps is an *atlas*. Both supply information about places.

Find the answers to these questions in a gazetteer or atlas.

1. In what state is Lake Winnipesaukee?
2. What is the latitude of Manila?
3. What state is directly north of Kansas?
4. Which is farther north, Rome, Italy or Denver, Colorado?
5. Which is larger in area, Canada or the U.S.?
6. What is the population of the five largest cities in the U.S.?
7. What is the area of your state? What is its rank in area among other states? in population? On what page is the map of your state?
8. What is the capital of Nebraska? of Kenya?
9. What is the population of the largest country in the world?

Books of Quotations

You may sometimes want to use the words of a famous author in your writing. Whether you know exactly what lines you want to quote or not, you will find what you need in books of quotations. *Bartlett's Familiar Quotations* indexes well known quotations by subject and author.

Use a Bartletts' or other reference to answer these questions.

1. Who wrote these words: "Talkers are no good doers"?
2. List two appropriate quotations you might use in a composition about courage. Who said or wrote them?
3. Find the rest of the quotation beginning, "A little learning is. . . ." Who wrote it? In what work?
4. Under what word in the index would you look to find who said, "The night has a thousand eyes"?
5. How many quotations are listed for Samuel Taylor Coleridge?

Biographical References

When you want to know something about the background of famous people, biographical references will supply you with short accounts of their lives. Some main ones are, *Biographical Dictionary, Current Biography, Who's Who* and *Who's Who in America*.

Consult one of the references named to find the answers.

1. What business is Mary Wells in?
2. What university did Thomas Jefferson design?
3. Name two plays written by Lillian Hellman.
4. What was the nickname of Thomas J. Jackson? Why was he so called?
5. What was Harry S. Truman's occupation before entering public office?
6. What state does Barbara Jordan represent in Congress?
7. What was John Glenn's main contribution as an astronaut?
8. Who is Julian Bond?
9. Where did Henry Kissinger receive his schooling?
10. What position did Gerald Ford play in college football?
11. Name four books written by Samuel L. Clemens.
12. Where was Gayle Sayers born?
13. What is Margaret Mead's specialty?
14. Who is Marilyn Horne?
15. Name three songs composed by Stephen Foster.

Periodical Indexes

Books usually take two years to publish. If you're looking for current thinking on your subject, you'll have to consult periodicals. The key to finding articles in magazines is the *Readers' Guide to Periodical Literature*, a set of references that indexes more than one hundred most-used magazines. You can find out which magazines are indexed by looking in the front of each volume. The years covered within each volume are printed on the spine. The most recent articles appear in thin paperback editions that are combined every few months before being bound into permanent larger volumes.

Using the sample entry for the *Readers' Guide*, find the following information.

1. If you were taking a course in cooking and had an assignment to do a presentation on vegetarian dishes, what articles listed on the sample page would you read?
2. What article(s) might help you plan an economy budget in a management course?
3. In a foods course, you are given the assignment to find as many ways as possible to prepare potatoes. What article might help you?
4. What article did Nathan H. Cook write? Where can it be found?
5. What is the subject of the four articles under Contracts—Saudi Arabia? Write the topic of a paper you might compose using these articles.
6. Under what other topic are you directed to look for more information on cookery?

Refer to the Key to Abbreviations and to the List of Periodicals Indexed at the front of the *Readers' Guide*. What do these abbreviations mean?

1. *Bsns W*
2. *abr*
4. *Pop Phot*
4. 63:14-33
5. *por* or *pors*
6. +
7. *Je*
8. *cond.*
9. *F*
10. *il*

CONTRACTS, Government—*Continued*
F-16 to employ 55,000-65,000 workers; list of major subcontracts planned and potential subcontractors. Aviation W 102:16 Ja 20 '75
General dynamics renews its Pentagon romance. il Bus W p58-9 F 3 '75
In love with "the sweet sixteen"; YF-16 contract to General dynamics. Fortune 91:21 F '75
Top 500 Defense dept. research and development contractors; tables. Aviation W 102:50-5 F 3 '75
YF-16 wins a dogfight. il Time 105:74 Ja 27 '75
See also
United States—Labor, Department of—Federal contract compliance, Office of

Saudi Arabia
Executive mercenaries; Vinnell corp. of Alhambra, Calif. hired to train Saudi Arabian forces. Time 105:16 F 24 '75
Mideast dilemma: is U.S. training a future foe? Vinnell contract. il U.S. News 78:21 F 24 '75
This gun for hire; Vinnell corporation's private army to train Saudi Arabian troops. K. Willenson and others. il Newsweek 85:30+ F 24 '75
Vinnell adds Saudis to its trainee roster. Bus W p28 F 24 '75

CONVECTION of heat. See Heat—Convection
CONVERTERS. See Electric current converters
COOK, Nathan H.
Computer-managed parts manufacture; with biographical sketch. il Sci Am 232:12, 22-9 bibl(p 114) F '75)
COOK, Richard L.
Gentleman (editor) from Verona. M. Jailer. il pors Ret Liv 15:26-8 F '75 •
COOK STRAIT swims. See Swimming
COOKBOOKS
Farm journal's new Country fair cookbook. E. W. Manning. il Farm J 99:48-50 F '75
COOKERY
Eating low off the hog. J. L. Hess and K. Hess. il Org Gard & Farm 22:99-103 F '75
Food (cont) A. Gold and R. Fizdale. Vogue 165:76+ F '75
Food questions you ask (cont) Am Home 78:40 F '75
How our food editors save money; with recipes. il McCalls 102:112-14+ F '75
Makings of a great cook; bride builds a repertoire of prized dishes. il Seventeen 34:128-31 F '75
Money saving guide; with recipes. Harp Baz 108:64-5 F '75
Prize winning recipes from thrifty cooks. D. Eby. il Bet Hom & Gard 53:78-85 F '75
Soy savy. il Bet Hom & Gard 53:46 F '75
Things you can't cook without the mixer; with recipes. il Ladies Home J 92:94-6 F '75
See also
Spreads (food)

Corn meal
Introduction to Italy's polenta. Sunset 154:114 F '75

Game
Armadillo à la mode; tastiest game meat in Florida. il Newsweek 85:54 Ja 27 '75
Crazy as a coot hunter; New England game with recipes. S. Moss. il Field & S 79:60-1+ F '75

Liquors
It will be bourbon's bicentennial, too; with recipes. W. P. Rayner. il House & Gard 147:93-5 F '75

Meat
Beef heart . . . on skewers or in stew. il Sunset 154:124 F '75
Daube de Boeuf; braised beef. J. Pépin. House B 117:80-1 F '75
Ham main dishes. il Bet Hom & Gard 53:89 F '75
Lower-cost meat cuts: how to cook them to perfection. il Good H 180:192 F '75

Nuts
Roasted nuts . . . from microwave. il Sunset 154:80 Ja '75

Organic food
Fitness house dish-of-the-month
Cashew carrot soup. il Org Gard & Farm 22:104-5 Ja '75
No-knead whole-wheat bread and Fitness house spread. il Org Gard & Farm 22:114-16 F '75

Rice
French way with rice; excerpt from From Julia's kitchen. J. Child. McCalls 102:66+ F '75

Shellfish
He cooks: oysters Lafitte. il Bet Hom & Gard 53:57 F '75

Vegetables
Dried beans: high-food value, low-cost favorites. R. Molter. il Parents Mag 50:50-4 Ja '75
How to find the flawless french fry. J. Villas. il Esquire 83:108-11 F '75
How to make a perfect salad and other delicious ways to serve vegetables; with recipes from Robert Dash. il House & Gard 147:87 F '75
International chef; the Famous' stuffed cabbage. D. Reynolds. Travel 143:72 F '75
Less meat, more vegetables for super value. M. Happel. il Am Home 78:62-3+ F '75
Not just for leftovers; stuffed vegetables. C. Claiborne and P. Franey. il N Y Times Mag p69 F 23 '75
Rediscover the potato: 20 quick recipes. J. Ellis. House & Gard 147:88+ F '75
Take a package of frozen potatoes. il Am Home 78:66+ F '75
There's always baked and boiled . . . ; potato recipes. C. Claiborne and P. Franey. il N Y Times Mag p54 Ja 19 '75

COOKERY, Caribbean
Melting pot; Creole or Gallo-Caribbean cuisine. R. Sokolov. il Natur Hist 84:98-100 Ja '75
COOKERY, French
Daube de Boeuf; braised beef. J. Pépin. House B 117:80-1 F '75
Pizza quiche. il Bet Hom & Gard 53:26 F '75
COOKERY, Indian (East Indian)
Dining in London, Indian style. T. Andrews. Holiday 56:35+ Ja '75
COOKERY, Italian
Anything goes—on pizza. il Seventeen 34:106-7+ F '75
Famous food from Venice; recipes from Harry's bar. A. Gold and R. Fizdale. Vogue 165:76+ F '75
Introduction to Italy's polenta. Sunset 154:114 F '75
COOKERY, Jewish
International chef; the Famous' stuffed cabbage. D. Reynolds. Travel 143:72 F '75
COOKERY, Lebanese
Lentil soups: your guests will cheer. il Sunset 154:108 F '75
COOKERY, Malaysian
It's soto soup . . . get in line. il Sunset 154:64-5 F '75
COOKERY, Marine
Hints on two-burner cooking. J. Groene. Motor B & S 135:34+ F '75
COOKERY, Middle East
See also
Cookery, Lebanese
COOKERY, Oriental
Ways to use hoisin sauce. il Sunset 154:122 F '75
COOKERY, Spanish
Three courses from one pot; *cocido*. il Sunset 154:48-9 Ja '75
COOKERY, Ukrainian
Hearty old-country soup; borsch with piroshki. il McCalls 102:87-8 F '75
COOLIDGE, Olivia (Ensor)
Writing about Abraham Lincoln; address, November 9, 1974. Horn Bk 51:31-5 F '75
COONEY, John Ducey
John D. Cooney: originality, scholarship, persistence. S. E. Lee. il por Art N 74:75 Ja '75 •
COONEY, Judd
New way to call coyotes. il pors Outdoor Life 155:50-2+ F '75
COOPER, Benjamin S. and Werthamer, N. R.
Two physicists on Capitol hill. il pors Phys Today 28:63-6 Ja '75
COOPER, Jon C. and Hasler, A. D.
Electroencephalographic evidence for retention of olfactory cues in homing coho salmon. bibl il Science 183:336-8; 187:82 Ja 25 '74, Ja 10 '75
COOPER, Richard N.
Invasion of the petrodollar. il Sat R 2:10-13 Ja 25 '75
COOPERATION
See also
Intercommunity cooperation
Religious cooperation
COOPERATION, Inter-American. See Inter-American relations
COOPERATIVE art galleries. See Art—Galleries and museums
COOPERATIVE associations
Food co-ops: for inflation-fighting savings! J. Wandres. il Ret Liv 15:24-7 Ja '75
COOPERATIVE education. See Education, Cooperative
COOT hunting
Crazy as a coot hunter; New England game with recipes. S. Moss. il Field & S 79:60-1+ F '75

Periodical Indexes

Articles are indexed in two ways—by subject and by author. Except for stories, magazine articles are not listed by title.

1. What articles on witchcraft and black magic appeared in 1972?
2. What articles on the same subject were published between 1907 and 1915?
3. *Newsweek, Time* and *Life* printed portraits of Frank Sinatra in the second half of 1943. In what issues of each magazine do the pictures appear? What is the title of each article carrying the pictures?
4. What articles on extrasensory perception were published between March '73 and February '74?
5. Select one of your hobbies. How many magazine articles published within the past year does the *Guide* list about this hobby? What are the titles and authors of two of these articles? In what magazines are they found? dates? page numbers?
6. Choose three of these topics and look up one article for each. Give complete information: title, author, magazine, date, page numbers.

    | The United Nations | Pollution | Education |
    | Atomic Energy | Medicine | Music |

7. Consult the list of magazines that your library subscribes to. Which articles that you found in question No. 6 above would you find in your library?
8. What articles has Norman Mailer published during the past month? the past year? the past two years?

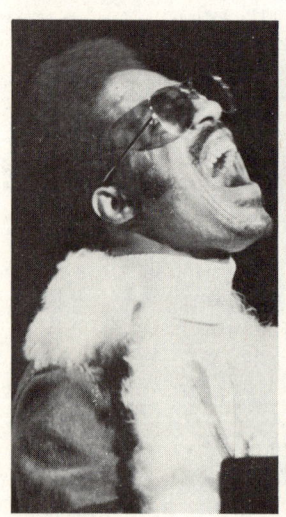

9. Select a subject you want to know more about—ESP, ecology, game shows. Find five articles that might be helpful in writing a paper on the topic. List all the information about each article.
10. Think of someone you are especially interested in. It might be a sports star, a foreign ruler or a TV or movie personality. Find three articles about the person. Search out and read the articles and formulate a theme topic that results from your reading. Use the pictures for ideas.

Vertical File

Every library clips newspaper items of special interest and files pamphlets, brochures and bulletins in a record called the *Vertical File*.

1. Where is the vertical file in your library? Can you personally have access to it or must you consult a librarian to use it?
2. What pamphlets are available on swamps and marshes? on other topics about environmental conservation?
3. What brochures from the Department of Agriculture are available? List some of the topics they cover.
4. Is there anything on UFO's? What?
5. What information does it contain about developments in your local community?

Records and Filmstrips

You may be asked to listen to a recording or view a filmstrip in preparation for a paper. Where are these audio-visuals indexed in your library—in the card catalogue or in a special file? If in a special file, where is the file located?

1. What are the call numbers of these records: "The Tragical History of the Life and Death of Doctor Faustus," and "Mozart, The Piano Quartets" performed by George Szell and the Budapest String Quartet?
2. Write the essential information about and the call numbers of three filmstrips and three records your library stores.

Microfilm, Microfiche, Microcard

Modern methods of photography make possible the economical storage of large amounts of material on film. *Microfilm* is on reels that are filed chronologically in drawers. *Microfiche* is sheets of film about the size of an index card and *microcards* are slightly larger cards that bear reduced photographs. Newspapers and magazines are popular subjects for this kind of storage. The *New York Times*, the *Chicago Tribune*, the *St. Louis Post-Dispatch* and *Newsweek* are a few items on microfilm.

Because of the newness of this method of storage, only a few newspapers and magazines have indexes of their contents. One of the most complete is the *New York Times Index* which provides easy access to almost every article printed in the late edition since the beginning of the paper in 1851.

1. At the beginning of each volume is a list of abbreviations used in the *Index*. Identify these:

OEO	ch	por
NORAD	Je	il
CATV	lr	S

2. The listings are strictly alphabetical. In which listing order would *CATV* appear?

cattuzza	Community and Social Agency
CATV	CATV
cauchefer	Community Centers

The *Index* presents abstracts of the news and editorial matter, abbreviating each reference in this order: date, page, column. A Roman numeral following the date indicates the Sunday section other than the news. Thus, My 6, IV, 3:4 means that the original article can be found in the May 6 edition, News of the Week in Review Section, page 3, column 4. To locate the article on microfilm, you must then consult the drawer containing the May 6 edition of the year of the volume containing the reference.

Excerpt from the *New York Times Index* © 1973 by The New York Times Company. Reprinted by permission.

> **TRANS Ocean Steel Corp. See also** Credit—US—Small Business, N 15. Steel—US, N 15
> **TRANSOHIO Financial Corp**
>   Union Financial and Transohio Financial agree in principle to merge to form one of largest savings and loan holding cos outside Calif, O 11,70:4
> **TRANSPLANTS. See also** disease and body part names
>   Symposium of 100 lawyers, drs and theoreticians meets to discuss legal questions posed by biomed advances in areas of organ transplants and artificial organs and behavior modification and control, Ja 28,50:4; Dr W T Summerlin on Mar 30 repts on laboratory tech that may make it possible to transplant organs without using dangerous immunity-suppressing drugs, rept to Amer Cancer Soc's 15th annual science writers seminar; has demonstrated approach in people who need grafts of skin, organ highly sensitive to rejection if transplanted between nonidentical individuals; method involves storing tissue that is to be transplanted for several wks in commericial solution that is used to grow tissues in laboratory flasks; Sommerlin says that after several wks, skin functions like fresh skin when transplanted to human; notes cultured skin was not rejected when transplanted to person who was genetically different from donor; says this occurs despite fact that original skin never lost its genetic 'foreignness' while in culture; experiments described; Summerlin notes that before findings can be applied to persons needing transplants or organs other than skin, further experimentation must be done; cites problem of inability to keep large, complex orgns such as kidneys and hearts alive in tissue cultures for more than a few days, Mr 31,50:1; correction story on Mar 31 story on human organ transplants notes Dr W T Summerlin recently moved to Sloan-Kettering Inst in NY, Ap 3,45:7

Using the excerpt of the *Index* printed here, answer the following.

1. How many articles were written in 1973 about transplants? What topics does Ja 28, 50:4 cover?

2. What is the cross reference to consult for more information on the Trans Ocean Steel Corporation? Include the subheads.

3. Where would you find the article on the merging of the Transohio Financial Corporation? What two corporations merged?

If you have access to other volumes, answer these questions.

1. In what issue and on what page of the *New York Times* can you find this article indexed in the 1929 volume, July-Dec.: "Ingres, Jean Auguste Dominique—Paintings and drawings"?

2. You know that 1929 was the year of the Wall Street crash. What directions are you given when you consult the topic, "Inflation"? When you follow the directives, what two sets of cross references are given? (See the beginning and end of the entry.) What two subheads other than U.S. are given? Where would you find a description for the new bills minted? How much did they amount to? How many were sent to South America? Where can you find an article on the story?

3. Which of the subject headings given below do you need to consult to find out when the article appeared announcing that Cleveland won the pennant and World Series in 1948? When did it appear?

   Indians   American League   World Series   Sports
   Cleveland   Baseball   Pennant   Professional Clubs

4. What was the largest attendance at a single game in baseball history in the World Series contest of 1948? Under what heading and subheads did you find this information?

5. Who was killed on July 15, 1973, falling off water skis in Jamaica Bay? Where did the article appear? What is the first name of the victim?

6. E. H. Hunt, Jr., pleaded guilty to the charges against him in the Watergate case sometime during the first two weeks of January 1973. On what exact day? When was the article about it printed? On what reel can you find the story?

7. In the first week of May, 1973 a newspaper won a prize for investigation of Watergate. On what day? Who were the recipients of the prize? What newspaper did they work for and when did the article appear? On what reel is the story stored?

8. Look up a topic you are interested in. What article was written about it? When?

Review: Write the name of the reference explained.

1. The index to all the books in a library.
2. You can discover whether the library has a particular book if you know one of three things. What are those three things?
3. The most useful index to magazines.
4. A system frequently used for arranging books on library shelves.
5. The book containing map, location, population and size of a place.

6. The quickest source of statistical information.
7. The most general reference books in the library.
8. The reference which lists the names of countries, cities, lakes and mountains alphabetically and gives their pronunciation.
9. A file of clippings, brochures and pamphlets.
10. A photographic means of storage which greatly reduces size.

Name the *best* library aid to use for finding each of the items listed below.

1. a picture of the pyramids of Egypt
2. sports record of an important athlete of the last three years
3. a synonym for "cold"
4. the height of Mount Fuji
5. the population of Denver
6. a brief biography of Eugene O'Neill, American playwright
7. a list of senators and representatives
8. the rest of the quotation beginning, "All the world's a stage. . . ."
9. the preferred pronunciation of *ration*
10. *West-Running Brook*, a book by Robert Frost
11. the book that catches up an encyclopedia on current topics
12. a recent article on American foreign policy
13. a specific article announcing the Supreme Court's latest ruling on capital punishment
14. a review of Doris Lessing's book *The Golden Notebook*
15. a filmstrip and record about mythology
16. the pronunciation of Kilimanjaro

WHO-DUNIT?

The basic unit of communication is the sentence. A sentence can be just two words or it can be a page long. Once you understand the structure of a sentence and know how to manipulate its parts, you have mastered English.

The sentence has two basic elements: a subject and a predicate. The subject is like the ending of a mystery movie; it answers the question everyone is asking: Whodunit? The **subject** tells who or what did the action stated in the sentence.

Nouns   57

A tenor sang.   The motorcycles fell.   Fran is sick.

Who sang? What fell? Who was sick? The subject tells you.

Because the subject of a sentence is usually a **noun,** you need to understand the workings of nouns. Think of nouns as names that identify persons, places, things or ideas. The nouns in the sample sentences are *tenor, motorcycles,* and *Fran.*

A reliable way to identify nouns is by inflections. **Inflections** are endings added to words to change the meaning somehow. Nouns can be inflected to be plural or possessive. The noun *motorcycles* has already been inflected to show plural — more than one motorcycle. The **plural** inflection is formed by adding **-s** or **-es** to the end of a noun.

The tenor**s** sang.   Echo**es** filled the valley.

The **possessive** is formed by adding **'s** to a singular noun and just an apostrophe to a plural noun.

The tenor**'s** voice is dramatic.   *singular possessive*

Tenor**s'** voices require training.   *plural possessive*

> Another name for determiners is noun markers.

You can often recognize nouns by the words that precede them. The number of nouns in English is uncountable, but there are only a few **determiners.** It is easy to remember them and try them out before a word you think may be a noun. They fall into five categories.

> See page 178.

Articles: **a** book, **an** apple, **the** cat

Possessive pronouns and nouns: **his** horse, **their** lunch, **Henry's** uncle

Demonstratives: **this** house, **that** street, **these** people, **those** cars

Indefinites: **all** children, **another** chance, **both** ideas, **each** person

Numbers: **seven** men, **three thousand** cannon

Find the noun subject in these sentences. Ask yourself who or what does the action of the sentence. One sentence has a two-noun subject.

1. Humpty Dumpty sat on the wall.
2. The other eggs stood below.
3. Humpty fell.
4. One egg was scrambled.
5. The king's horses came.
6. His men came too.
7. Both the horses and the men couldn't reconstitute H. D.
8. An egg was gone.
9. The cavalry retreated.
10. The story is ended.

Pronouns

Pronouns, too, can be subjects of sentences. A pronoun takes the place of a noun. Only certain pronouns can be subjects. They include the personal pronouns: *I*, *you*, *he*, *she*, *it*, *we*, *they*, and the indefinite pronouns when they are not followed by a noun.

Ken ran. **He** ran.

Ken and Barbie ran. **They** ran.

Both Ken and Barbie ran. **Both** ran.

Identify the subject in each sentence below. Watch out for indefinites functioning as determiners.

1. In the morning we had toast and coffee.
2. It rained last night.
3. Are you crazy?
4. They came for us in gleaming white wagons.
5. Then you must be mad!
6. All came running to see.
7. They arranged themselves along the wall.
8. Each man held his breath.

9. Everyone breathed heavily.
10. I cannot help you now.

You should recognize other nouns in some of the sentences you just worked with. Keep in mind that categories such as "noun" and "pronoun" are form classes or parts of speech. The category "subject of a sentence" describes a word's function in relation to other words in a sentence. You will review the function of the other nouns in a sentence later.

Compounds

The subject of a sentence can also be compound—that is, more than one subject.

Bob and Ray went to Alaska.

The compound subject is *Bob and Ray*, two people performing the same action. Remember that only the pronouns *I, you, he, she, it* and *they* can be subjects. Don't be confused if a pronoun is part of a compound subject; it must still be one of the subject pronouns.

Identify the compound subjects in these sentences and decide which pronoun should be used.

I, me   1. Hal and ____ will be late.

He, Him   2. ____ and Betty will be on time, however.

they, them   3. In the twilight, the campers and ____ sat by the lake.

She, Her
we, us   4. ____ and ____ are leaving soon.

we, us   5. They and ____ care about you.

They, Them   6. ____ and their lawyers arrived early.

I, me   7. Mrs. Columbo and ____ will help.

He, Him
I, me   8. ____ and ____ are in the last row.

she, her   9. Are you and ____ ready?

The Latest Thing

"The Merry Singer" does not refer to a vocalist. What does it refer to? What do you think the purpose of this song was?

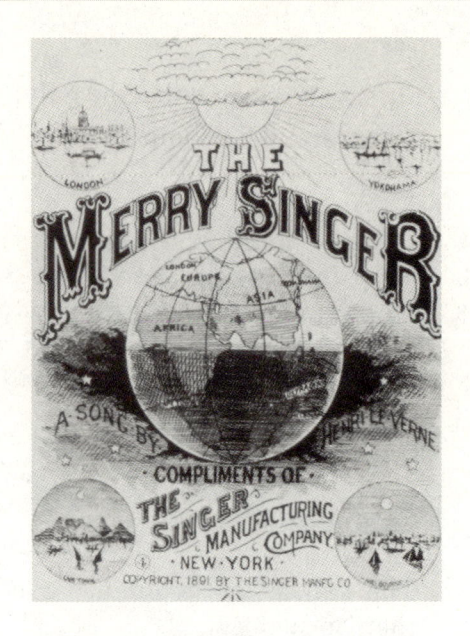

The Merry Singer

Where the sun is beaming,
There you'll hear my song,
For I'm widely scattered, Ev'rywhere belong;
E'en when you are spinning
With the globe thro' night,
I am somewhere singing
In the golden light.
I am a singer, I am a singer—
I'm a merry singer I am a singer—
I'm a merry singer, Singing for you!

I am heard in Russia, France and sunny Spain;
In the smoke of London I am heard again;
All the wide world over, Look where-e'er you may,
You will find me busy
Singing ev'ry day.

Ev'ry lady likes me,
Once she hears me sing,
For she knows I ever
Ease and comfort bring;
Home I make the brighter
By the good I do,
And, if you but ask me,
I will sing for you.

VERBUM EST

The word *verb* comes from the Latin word *verbum* which means "word." And the verb *is* the important word in the sentence. Nouns are identifiers—names for things—but verbs carry the action; they tell what's going on.

Verbs, too, can be recognized by their inflections. All verbs have a simple form, sometimes called the infinitive form, with no special ending: *walk, see, do*. The other two inflections that all verbs have are:

Third person singular or -*s* form: he walk**s**, she see**s**, it doe**s**

Past tense or -*ed* form: walk**ed**, saw, did

The third person singular form is used only with the third person singular pronouns (he, she, it) and with singular nouns. The past tense form takes the inflection *-d* or *-ed* with all regular verbs: *walked, scored*. But notice that two of the examples are irregular verbs: *saw, did*. Many of the most common verbs are irregular. They are so common in fact that you do not need to study the forms; you use them without hesitation.

The most irregular verb in English is *be*. The forms of *be* are:

I	am, was	we	are, were
you	are, were	you	are, were
he, she, it	is, was	they	are, were

Try to identify the changes you are making.

Rewrite each sentence below following the directions in parentheses. Change the verb to fit.

1. An ant drowns in water. (Add *yesterday*.)
2. My gloves fit well. (Change *gloves* to *glove*.)
3. Marty dives from the side of the pool. (Add *this morning*.)
4. I think you are trustworthy. (Change *are* to *were*.)
5. A spelling error occurs in your paper. (Change to *three spelling errors*.)

6. I try to make a living for my family. (Substitute *she* for *I*.)
7. I got up early this morning. (Change to *every morning*.)
8. Bob ate dinner earlier. (Change *Bob* to *they*.)
9. He washes the dishes too. (Change *he* to *they*.)
10. The old door creaks. (Add *as we walked in*.)

Problems arise with the second major identifying factor for verbs, the use of auxiliaries. **Auxiliaries** are sometimes called helping verbs. They help the main verb express other times and conditions. Auxiliaries are used with specific forms of the verb and often with special inflections.

The first group of auxiliaries are modals. **Modals** are used with the simple form of the verb. The modals are: *can, could, shall, should, will, would, may, might, must, do, did* and *does.*

I shall go later.

You must know the answer.

Dave will help you.

The second auxiliary includes all the forms of **have:** *has, have, had.* The auxiliary *have* is followed by the verb inflection known as the **past participle.** Regular verbs use the *-ed* form for both the past tense form and the past participle form.

I walk**ed** home.

I **have** walk**ed** home every night.

I **had** arriv**ed** before they left.

But irregular verbs usually take a different form. It may be the same as the past tense form of the irregular verb, or it may be completely different.

I **hit** the ball.   I **have hit** a home run.

She **took** the picture.   She **has taken** many pictures.

Auxiliaries

The last kind of auxiliary includes the forms of **be:** *am*, *are*, *is*, *was* and *were*. This auxiliary is followed by the *-ing* or **participle** form of the verb.

Selma **is** swing**ing** the bat.

Arthur and his friends **are** com**ing** later.

To avoid confusion, think of the *be* and *have* auxiliaries as completely different words from the verbs *be* and *have*. Since you can use both the auxiliary and the verb together, you can see that they are functionally different words.

aux v   **aux v**
I have had the flu.   He is being ornery.

The auxiliaries can be used together to express different times and conditions. When they are used together, they follow a very regular order: **1** modal, **2** have, **3** be. Each auxiliary determines the form of the word that follows it. The modal is always followed by the simple form, *have* by the past participle form, and *be* by the participle form.

She **will see** you now.   modal + simple form of verb

She **will have seen** you already.   modal + simple form of *have* + past participle form of *see*

He **has gone** to bed.   *have* + past participle form of verb

He **has been going** to bed for hours.   *have* + past participle form of *be* + participle form of *go*

Since the order is so regular, you probably rarely have problems with auxiliaries and verbs. However, you need to know the order so that you can avoid a few potential errors you will study later.

Write the verb phrase you would use for each sentence below. Follow this code: M = modal, H = have, B = be, V = verb.

break   1. Rodney HV the window.

lie   2. The insect M H V in the spore state for years.

64   Verbs

loose	3. You M V me now.
ring	4. Bella M H V the bell.
weave	5. Uncle Will H V a rug.
lose	6. I M H V my car keys.
practice	7. That violinist M H B V for years.
fly	8. The convicts B V down the back alley.
speak	9. Regina H just V to her husband.
prove	10. Walter M H V right after all.

Trouble Spots

The first troublesome area in the use of verb forms is a simple sound problem. Some people mistakenly use *of* for the contraction of *have*.

   I might've known you'd quit.   **not**   might of

This happens because the two words sound exactly alike when you are speaking. However, you should recognize that the auxiliary *have* is the only word that makes sense before a verb; a preposition (*of*) does not.

Correct the have-of error in these sentences if necessary. Identify the past participle form of the verb after *have*.

1. Jim should of ordered shakes for us.
2. I asked Rachel if she would of liked one.
3. Nan might of had a chocolate shake.
4. In fact, I wouldn't have refused one myself.
5. I could of killed him for not asking us.
6. He must of known we were hungry.
7. You could've told me he was stingy.
8. I would of had vanilla.

   The other potential error is using the wrong form of the verb—especially choosing between the past tense form and the past participle form for use with the auxiliary *have*. The best way to correct this error is by practice.

Write down on your paper the form of the verb you would use in each sentence below. If you are not sure of the spelling, look in the dictionary under the simple form of the verb. It will tell you the spelling of the other forms.

put	1. The faculty have ___ on quite a show.
see	2. Who has ___ the wind?
tease	3. They ___ the winner unmercifully.
be	4. Have you ___ to Rio?
fly	5. We ___ down last year.
cost	6. Did it ___ a lot?
cost	7. It ___ more than we expected.
freeze	8. Walter has ___ the leftovers.
freeze	9. I almost ___ waiting for you.
go	10. Alma and Betty ___ to Cape Cod.
take	11. Alma ___ her dog with her.
drive	12. Betty ___ most of the way.
read	13. Alma ___ the signs and maps.
eat	14. Betty said they had both ___ lobster every night.
hurt, fall	15. Chris ___ his arm when he ___ off the swing.
breathe, bring	16. We ___ a sigh of relief when they ___ in the cake.
speak	17. I have ___ to your daughter.
lie	18. He ___ down for half an hour.
lay	19. Roger has ___ the baby in his crib.
shrink	20. Has that sweater ___?
write	21. Angela has ___ a novel.
tear	22. He ___ the wrapping away.
hold	23. Mrs. Ortiz has ___ that job for several years.
sit	24. The speaker ___ with his back to us.
wear	25. You have ___ that skirt every day this week.
rent	26. The Masons have ___ that house.
become, learn	27. He had ___ a star before he ___ how to act.

MODIFICATION

Adjectives and adverbs are two kinds of words you must be able to recognize and handle. They have similar functions—to modify or alter the meaning of other words. Adjectives modify nouns. *Red* motorcycles are different from *green* ones. *Red* describes the color of the cycle. Other adjectives might describe it in other ways: *expensive, old-fashioned, glistening, noisy, large*. No matter how adjectives describe nouns, they answer the question: What kind of?

See page 57 for noun markers.

Adjectives precede nouns; if there is a noun marker, they occur between the noun marker and the noun.

n-m	adj	n
the	yellow	curtains

Find all the adjectives in this paragraph.

The four young men lounged around the worn, wooden table, sipping cold beer. From time to time, a tall, lanky boy pounded his large fist on the shaky table to emphasize a point. A sleepy-eyed, fat youth held his rolling head in one pudgy hand and a dripping can in the other. Directly under the blue light, a third sweated great drops as he argued his point. The fourth member only watched. Silent and tense, he seemed ready to pounce.

See page 61 or page 80 for forms of be.

Adjectives also occur after forms of the verb *be*. In this position they refer to the subject of the sentence.

Curly is *hungry*.

The contestants are *nervous*.

Hungry refers to *Curly* and *nervous* describes the *contestants*. Occasionally adjectives will appear after the noun they modify when a writer wants to emphasize them.

The new president, cool and deliberate, opened the meeting.

Adjectives 67

Identify all the adjectives in the first three sentences. They may occur before or after nouns or after a form of *be*. In the last two sentences, supply adjectives wherever there is a blank.

1. The sailor's curly red beard was flecked with iridescent drops of sea spray.
2. The big, brawny athlete was really soft-hearted, gentle and shy.
3. The refugee was only a child, hungry, frightened and alone.
4. As a gas station attendant, Miriam was ____ and ____.
5. The ____, ____ steamboat waited at the pier, ____ and ____.

Because adjectives describe, they are used for comparisons.

> Mrs. Kennedy's hair is **long.**
> Mrs. Onassis' hair is **longer.**
> Caroline's hair is **longest** of all.

How would you change the adjectives in these sentences to show comparison?

> The Terminal Tower is a tall building. (No comparison)
>
> The Empire State Building is *tall* than the Terminal.
>
> But the Sears Tower is the *tall* building of all.

Adjectives

When you compare *two* things you use the comparative form adding -er. When you compare *more than two* things, you use the superlative form, adding -est. This rule applies to all one-syllable words and to many two-syllable words. Notice that sometimes the final consonant is doubled when the word is inflected: *mad, madder, maddest*. Some two-syllable words show comparison by adding *more, most* or *less, least*, instead of -er and -est. When you are in doubt about which form to use, check a dictionary.

    twisted   more twisted   most twisted

    kindly   less kindly   least kindly

Some adjectives can use either form.

    handsome   more handsome   most handsome

    handsome   handsomer   handsomest

Adjectives of more than two syllables always use *more, most, less, least* rather than -er and -est endings.

    beautiful   more beautiful   most beautiful

A few adjectives have individual inflections.

good, well	better	best
bad, ill	worse	worst
little	smaller (size)	smallest
little	less (amount)	least
few	less	least
much, many	more	most
far	farther (distance)	farthest
far	further (time)	furthest

You won't have trouble forming comparisons if you remember to choose either the *-er* form or *more*, **not both;** either the *-est* form or *most*. Why is *more worser* illogical?

Form the comparisons called for in these sentences.

1. Stella is (young) than her brother Bert.
2. Yesterday her fever was (bad) than it is today.
3. This is the (bad) cold I've ever had.
4. Coletta is the (humble) person I know.
5. Miss Nelson's bulletin board is (elaborate) than yours.
6. Do you live (near) to Juan or to Tony?
7. The stock market averages are the (high) they've ever been.
8. Tom is the (thin) of the three men.
9. Of the two plans, this one is (practical). It is definitely inferior.
10. Tiny is the (timid) of the riders.

More Modifiers

What word modifies the subject noun in this sentence?

The galloping horse broke stride.

You should recognize that *galloping* is modifying *horse*. The *-ing* ending also tells you that the word *galloping* is the participle form of the verb. Both the participle and the past past participle form can function like adjectives. You won't confuse them with verbs if you remember that they need auxiliaries in order to function as verbs.

The horse **is** gallop**ing**.

The horse **has** gallop**ed**.

Identify all the participles in these sentences and tell what noun each participle modifies.

1. The cheering throng greeted the returning team.
2. A wasted opportunity is gone forever.
3. Smiling sweetly, Deborah slammed the door.

4. An opened package stood on the table.
5. Dancing wildly, Regis dropped to the floor.
6. Bored and tired, Amy got up to leave.
7. A fluttering flag waved over our heads.
8. Pulling and tugging, she hauled the fish in.
9. An old dress, faded and worn, was all she had.
10. Dancing and singing raucously, the chorus made its entrance.

Adverbs share many characteristics with adjectives, but they differ in one major way. Adverbs modify verbs primarily.

Regis danced wildly.

Wildly does not change the meaning of the noun *Regis*, so it is not an adjective. But it does change the verb *danced*. Dancing *wildly* is different from dancing *slowly*. *Wildly* tells how Regis danced. Adverbs answer these questions:

How: Mari sang **cheerfully.**

When: Isabel worked **late.**

To what extent: John **hardly** touched his dinner.

Where: Please come **here.**

Write one adverb for each of these verbs. Tell which question the adverb answers.

writes   cheers   watches   sings   reads

listens   ran   pounced   tossed   escaped

Adverbs can modify adjectives and other adverbs as well as verbs.

adjective: He walked around in a **mildly** confused state.
adverb: We are **very** distantly related.

The adverbs *very, quite, somewhat,* and *rather* are also called **intensifiers.** Generally speaking it is better to choose a forceful adverb or adjective than a weak one and an intensifier. Adverbs have these other characteristics:

1. They are often formed by adding *-ly* to an adjective. (Don't assume that all words ending in *-ly* are adverbs; *friendly,* for example, is not.)
2. They can sometimes be inflected to show comparison in the same way adjectives can: *quietly, more quietly, most quietly.*
3. Adverbs that modify verbs can often move around in a sentence.

>*Stealthily*, he edged toward the door.
>
>He edged toward the door *stealthily*.
>
>He edged *stealthily* toward the door.

One group of adverbs have the power to change the meaning of verbs from positive to negative: *not, never, hardly, scarcely, barely.* The rule is that only one negative word is allowed in a sentence. Some other negative words are:

>**noun marker:** no
>
>**pronouns:** nobody, no one, nothing, none

A sentence such as *I can't find nothing to fit me* has two negatives — *n't* and *nothing*. It must give up one negative to read correctly.

Rewrite these sentences to eliminate one negative.

1. Harvey didn't scarcely listen to the music.
2. Doesn't Alma want no pie?
3. She said she doesn't want none.
4. I don't want nothing to go wrong.
5. There wasn't hardly anybody in the hall.
6. Nobody don't want your help.
7. Didn't you want nothing for lunch?

Prepositional Phrases

The adjectives and adverbs you have met so far have all been one word:

A *white* car drove by the house.

Carefully, Beulah peeled the grape.

Sometimes groups of words can function like adjectives and adverbs. Any word group that works as a unit but does not have a subject and predicate is a **phrase.**

adjective: A white car *with blue fenders* drove by the house.

adverb: Beulah peeled the grape *with care*.

With blue fenders describes the noun *car* in the same way that the single adjective *white* does. Because it does not have a subject and predicate, it is not a sentence, but it does have a regular structure that identifies it as a prepositional phrase.

prep. adj. noun

with blue fenders

Prepositional phrases always begin with a preposition and close with a noun. They may include determiners and adjectives, but those elements are optional. A prepositional phrase may function like an adjective to describe a noun, or it may modify a verb as an adverb does. The phrase *with care* tells **how** Beulah peeled the grape and modifies *peeled*. The most common prepositions are these:

at	for	of	through
after	from	off	to
before	in	on	under
by	into	onto	up
down	near	out	with

Make three columns on your paper. In the first write the subject of each sentence below; in the second, write the preposition that begins each prepositional phrase, and in the third, write the noun that ends the phrase.

1. Frank used the sandpaper on the big oak desk.
2. The students in this special class are admirers of Beethoven.
3. Geraldo has read a play by Shakespeare.
4. The store down the street sells six packs of Coors beer.
5. A girl in a white helmet rode the last cycle to the finish line.
6. They gave the prize to the man with the longest beard.
7. Sylvia danced in the basement.
8. Among the garbage cans, rats romped freely.
9. The box of candy was filled with nougats.
10. A man in a raincoat will meet you under the street light at midnight.

Another kind of phrase that functions like an adjective is the **participle phrase.** You have already studied single participles modifying nouns: A *tattered* coat, a *penetrating* glance. Participle phrases modify nouns just as single participles do, but they include other words or word groups.

> *Telling the truth at last,* Jed felt relieved.
>
> She heard her cousin *whistling in the shower.*

The participle phrase in the first sentence modifies the noun *Jed*; that in the second sentence modifies *cousin*. If a participle phrase occurs first in a sentence, it is set off by a comma.

Identify the participle phrases and the nouns they modify in these sentences.

1. Building a boat in a bottle, Mike whiled away his hours.
2. Having slipped on the peel, he broke his leg.
3. He broke his leg slipping on a peel.

4. Beaten by their opponents, the Cougars lost the championship.
5. Turning to his wife, Mark whispered the time.

Both prepositions and participles may be followed by pronouns as well as nouns.

participle: Seeing the ship, Mari jumped for joy.
Seeing **it,** Mari jumped for joy.

preposition: The baby ran to Edgar.
The baby ran to **him.**

See page 78 for more uses of object pronouns.

Note that the pronouns that can function as subject of the sentence are different words from those that can follow prepositions and participles. The object pronouns—those that follow prepositions and participles—are *me, you, her, him, it, us, them.* Don't be confused by a compound structure; the pronoun must still be the same.

Seeing Jane and Al, we waved.

Seeing her and him, we waved.

Try them separately to be sure: *Seeing her, we waved.* (You would not say *Seeing she.* . . .) *Seeing him, we waved.* (You would not say *Seeing he.* . . .)

Choose the correct pronoun for each sentence.

he, him	1. They gave the grades to ____ .
he, him	2. They gave the grades to Rachel and ____ .
she, her	3. Watching ____ on the trampoline, we were impressed.
we, us	4. The team walked by the coach and ____ without looking.
she, her	5. To the travellers, Bob and ____ looked exotic.
we, us	6. Discovering ____ under the stairs, they called the doctor.
they, them we, us	7. Give the last pieces to ____ and ____ .

One problem to be aware of with participles is making sure they have a noun to modify. For example:

Singing at the top of his lungs, the dogs cringed in pain.

Singing at the top of his lungs here modifies *dogs,* but the dogs aren't singing. This dangling participle phrase can be converted in this way.

Singing at the top of his lungs, Chuck saw the dogs cringe in pain.

Now *singing* modifies the noun *Chuck,* the word it relates to.

Correct any modifiers that do not have a noun to modify. If the sentence is correct, write C.

1. Dialing a prayer, the agency answered the telephone at once.
2. Shining brightly in the sky, the moon glowed.
3. Handling the deck with skill, Rose easily slipped the ace to the bottom.
4. Handling the deck with ease, the players noticed that Rose had slipped an ace to the bottom.
5. Having awakened him at four, Harry was annoyed at the roosters.
6. Smoking from his nostrils, St. George killed the dragon.
7. Having finished dinner, the dishes were washed.
8. After receiving my license, my father let me drive the car.
9. Reading the evening papers, my meal was not very festive.
10. The thoughtful girl appreciated the symphony paying close attention to the music.
11. Born in Stratford, the last days of Shakespeare's life were spent in the town of his birth.
12. After sewing on the button, the sleeves of the blouse split.
13. Knowing his temperament, the horse was easily mastered.
14. Bored with television, the new series did not interest me.

Participle Phrases

Combine these sentences into tightly knit statements that include a participle phrase.

1. The horse was whinnying piteously. It crashed into the gate.
2. The mountains melted into the mist. They were ringed with soft, rolling vapor.
3. Ned dangled his participles in every sentence. He failed his English course.
4. The argument ended as abruptly as it had begun. It had become hot and heated.
5. Carmella awoke several times during the night. The cars on the main highway had disturbed her slumber.

Finish these by supplying a noun-subject and a verb to follow. Don't forget the comma.

1. Wiping the perspiration from his forehead with a large red hanky
2. Kneeling in the dust beside the car
3. Crouching in the corner in the dark
4. Having eaten too fast
5. Cleaning the attic

Write participle phrases to modify the italicized words.

1. The *ant* lay half dead.
2. *Marge* came in the front door.
3. *Pete* found a silver *dollar*.
4. *Aaron* watched his *house*.
5. *Irene* put the frying *pan* into the water.

UNDERPINNINGS

The simplest complete sentence you can write is only two words —one subject noun and one predicate verb. These two elements are the underpinnings of everything you write.

S-n   **P-v**
Garbage   smells.

Even a one-word command such as "Leave!" has the understood subject *you*. Your range of expression would be severely limited if you never wrote sentences of more than two words. And many kinds of nouns and verbs cannot stand alone. Verbs such as *smells*, which can stand alone, are called **intransitive;** other verbs, however, require an object, a noun to receive the action they describe. For example, the verb *give* requires an object.

Regis gives blood once a year.

The object of the verb *gives* is the noun *blood*. A verb that takes an object is called **transitive.** The object completes the action of the verb.

Angela drinks coffee in the morning.

The noun *coffee* completes the idea of drinking and tells you what Angela drinks.

All of the following sentences follow the pattern Subject-Transitive Verb-Direct Object. In three columns on your paper, identify those three elements for each sentence.

1. The horse kicked the bucket of oats.
2. For this the farmer whipped him.
3. The horse left the barn.
4. The farmer replaced the oats.
5. Fresh oats awaited the horse's return.

Take another look at page 74.

The object of a transitive verb can be a pronoun as well as a noun.

I hate him.

Just as only certain pronouns can be subjects of sentences, only these pronouns can be objects: *me, you, him, her, it, us* and *them*. When there is only one object after a transitive verb, using the right pronoun comes automatically. But don't be confused by compounds.

The same pronouns are used even when the objects are compound, as in this sentence.

Reuben took him and me.

Compare this with page 59.

The easiest way to check your pronoun choice is to break down the compound object into two separate statements that will clearly show which pronoun to use.

Reuben took him. (*You'd never say* Reuben took he.)

Reuben took me. (*You'd never say* Reuben took I.)

Choose the correct pronoun for each sentence below.

I, me	1. The cast chose Hazel and ____.
he, him	2. Stanley and ____ will need help.
I, me	3. Preston and ____ want you and ____ now.
he, him	
I, me	4. Sam has invited you and ____.
she, her	5. Dawn and ____ watched the show.
she, her	6. They called on Dawn and ____.
they, them	7. The coach asked to see ____ and ____.
we, us	
he, him	8. Coming in late, Tony and ____ slammed the door.
they, them	9. Verne and ____ asked Bob and ____ to the party.
we, us	
we, us	10. You and ____ will arrive early.

Be Verbs

Another kind of sentence structure involves the verb *be* or a verb that can be replaced by *be*.

Lily is nervous.

Elaine is the new president.

Justin appears confused.

In these sentences, the verb links the subject with either a noun or an adjective (called a *predicate nominative* and *predicate adjective*). It makes them equal.

The main linking verb is *be* and all its forms: *am, are, is, was, were, been, being*. Verbs that can function as linking verbs are:

>   act (stupid)   look (miserable)
>
>   appear (uneasy)   remain (cool)
>
>   become (hysterical)   run (wild)
>
>   feel (worn)   seem (wrong)
>
>   get (sick)   sound (angry)
>
>   go (mad)   taste (good)

These verbs can often function as action words as well.

>   I smelled the pickles.

Obviously *pickles* is not equal to *I*. But in *The pickles smelled sour, sour* is equal to *pickles*. You can identify verbs other than *be* as linking verbs if you can **1.** substitute a form of *be* for them **2.** judge whether they make the subject and the adjective or noun following it equal to each other.

>   I think I am going mad.   I = mad

>   We followed closely.

You cannot say *we* = *closely*. *Closely* refers to the verb and is an adverb.

>   The room felt close.

You can readily say *close room* or *room* = *close*. In this case *close* refers to *room*, and *felt* is a linking verb. If the word following the linking verb is not a noun, it must be an adjective, not an adverb.

Linking Verbs 81

In the following sentences, decide whether the verbs are linking verbs. If they are, write the adjective form; if they are not, write the adverb form.

1. This book seems (heavy, heavily) for its size.
2. I feel (bad, badly) about that oversight.
3. The accident was (sudden, suddenly).
4. This soup tastes (good, well).
5. The team played (good, well).
6. Wilbur sounded (distant, distantly) over the phone.
7. The band director looked (angry, angrily) at the trumpeter.
8. You look (ridiculous, ridiculously) in that hat.
9. You should drive (careful, carefully).
10. Don't act so (innocent, innocently).
11. She feels (terrible, terribly) tonight.
12. Doesn't that singer sound (flat, flatly)?
13. Isn't it a bit (sudden, suddenly) for a marriage?
14. He grew (red, redly).
15. He grew (quick, quickly).

Because the subject and complement are equal when they are joined by a linking verb, a pronoun following a linking verb should be the subject form to agree with the subject.

>Are you the manager? *I* am *he*.

These are the subject pronouns: *I, you, he, she, it, we, they*. You may be tempted to forget which pronouns to use when you are writing a compound predicate nominative. That is because in speaking you would probably say:

>The winners are Val and *him*.

But writing requires more care. The correct form is:

>The winners are Val and *he*. (Not *him*, because both words are equal to the subject and must be in the subject form.)

Decide whether the verbs in these sentences are action or linking verbs. Then write in the correct pronoun forms: subject if the pronouns are predicate nominative, and object if they are objects of the verb or of a preposition.

1. The losers are Jesse and (she, her).
2. Tell Matt and (me, I) what happened.
3. Can these charming children be Ardis and (I, me)?
4. No, they appear to be Ardis and (she, her).
5. Flanking the house are the dogs on one side and (we, us) on the other.
6. Give (they, them) all the help they need.
7. The winners are Matt and (she, her).
8. It is (he, him) who has ruined the garden.
9. You saw (I, me) earlier today.
10. That product has helped (they, them) with their arthritis.

COMPOUND INTEREST

You're fairly sure you can identify the elements of a simple sentence now, aren't you? Test yourself. Which is a sentence, which is not?

> In the evening, sitting by the campfire with the flames casting flickering shadows on the faces of all.

> Jordan met the horses at the river.

You should have had no trouble recognizing that there is the unanswered question in the first word group, *Who was sitting by the campfire?* Whodunit, in other words. The subject is missing. But you could immediately identify the subject and verb in the second example. That is the secret—any group of words that makes sense by itself and has a subject and verb is a simple sentence.

You can now feel confident to go on to more complicated sentences. One of these is the compound sentence. It has two complete and independent sentences joined by a special joining word called a *coordinating conjunction*. Find the two sentences in this compound sentence:

> Jordan met the horses at the river, but they were not able to cross.

The word groups joined in a compound sentence are called clauses. A clause is a group of words that contains a subject and a verb and is part of a sentence. A clause that can stand alone is called an **independent** clause. The parts of a compound sentence are independent clauses.

There are only six coordinating conjunctions: *and, but, or, nor, for, yet*. But watch out before you call a sentence compound. Don't confuse a compound subject or a compound predicate with a compound sentence.

You can review compound subjects on page 59.

> **S + S   V + V**
> Jessie and Jude ran and jogged all day.

When the conjunction falls between the two subjects or between the two verbs, the sentence is still simple because you cannot split it into two separate sentences.

> Jessie and Jude   Ran and jogged.

A true compound sentence can be split into two complete sentences.

> **S   V   S   V**
> Jessie ran,   and   Jude jogged all day.

More about this on page 135.

Notice that a comma is placed after the first clause just before the coordinating conjunction to separate the two clauses. Write one compound sentence using any of the coordinating conjunctions. Don't forget the comma to separate the clauses.

Another way to create a compound sentence is to join two independent, closely related clauses by a semicolon.

> The machine is jammed; it will only take quarters.

Write three sentences based on these photos using the semicolon as a joiner. Be sure the clauses are related in meaning. This one isn't.

The machine is jammed; Bombay is a hot city.

Tell whether these sentences are simple or compound by putting appropriate words under these column headings. If each column has an entry, the sentence is compound.

    subject   verb   conjunction or semicolon   subject   verb

1. Grape hyacinths are among the earliest flowers in spring, for they do not die in snow.
2. Tulips and hyacinths are the next to blossom.
3. Shortly after, the daffodils and jonquils bloom; they brighten the fields with color.
4. In mid-May, azaleas bloom, and then their relatives the rhododendrons appear.
5. Fruit blossoms pop out next, but lilacs are not far behind.
6. Near June, lilacs and spirea, or bridal wreath, fill the air with perfume and white lace.
7. Meanwhile roses of every variety bud; they include floribundas and hybrid teas.
8. Climbing roses transform old barns into a riot of color, for they shoot out half a dozen blooms on a single stem.
9. After roses come the many common garden plants like petunias, geraniums and marigolds.
10. Finally, summer arrives full strength with glads and zinnias, but you must wait till late August for asters and mums.

    A third way to join independent clauses into compound sentences is by a special joining adverb used with a semicolon.

    Large cars are luxurious; **however,** they consume lots of gas.

The adverb can come first as it does in the sentence above, or it can appear later in the second clause.

    Large cars are luxurious; they consume lots of gas, **however.**

In both cases a semicolon separates the clauses. The joining adverb is set off by commas, especially if it interrupts the flow of the second clause.

Some of the joining adverbs are:

Result	Addition	Exception or Contrast	Alternative
consequently	also	however	at the same time
hence	besides	nevertheless	on the other hand
therefore	furthermore	nonetheless	moreover
thus	indeed	still	otherwise
	for example	yet	
	too		

Write an original sentence using one of the joining adverbs and a semicolon.

Decide which of the three available ways would be best to join these simple sentences into compound sentences.

1. Every painter knows that green is a difficult color to reproduce. It is either too bright or too dull to use straight from the tube.
2. One way to create a different green is by blending orange and green. This gives a warm but drab olive.
3. A green close to black but more alive is made by mixing red and green. You must be careful not to overdo this melancholy shade.
4. Green and yellow, of course, make warm yellow-greens. They will create a mood of early spring on your canvas.
5. Amateurs are tempted to mix black with green to darken it. This will only deaden the color and reduce the liveliness of any scene.

See page 138 in the punctuation chapter.

Keep in mind that you cannot join two independent clauses with a comma alone unless they are very short.

wrong: Everyone gathered around the man on the soapbox, he began distributing leaflets.

right: Everyone gathered around the man on the soapbox; he began distributing leaflets.

or: Everyone gathered around the man on the soapbox, and he began distributing leaflets.

This error is known as a comma splice or a run-on sentence.

Correct any run-on sentences in this paragraph.

Is skiing an exciting sport? Once you've mastered the basics, it can be challenging especially if you enter racing competition. The starter shouts, "It's time"! And the pressure of winning is on in slalom, a downhill skiing race over a zigzag course, the skiers must turn around gates placed close together, in giant slalom the gates are farther apart but speeds are greater. In downhill racing speeds can reach 70 m.p.h., imagine a spill traveling at that rate. It's important to be sure your binding releases are perfectly adjusted. If you fall at high speeds and your skis don't come off, you could get pretty badly mangled, just thinking about the danger makes me tingle with equal parts of fear and delight. You ask if it's really worth it to put your life in such danger, what can I say? You have to try it yourself, then you'll know.

UNDERSTANDING CLAUSES IS A COMPLEX MATTER

The one-word adjective and the adjective phrase are familiar to you.

word   A *white* car drove by the house.

phrase   A car *with blue fenders* drove by the house.

Once you understand and can recognize adjectives, it's no problem to identify the adjective clause; it functions the same way—modifying a noun.

clause   A car *which was white with blue fenders* drove by the house.

The adjective clause *which was white with blue fenders* modifies the noun *car*. A clause, as you know, contains a subject and a verb. The subject here is *which* and the verb is *was*. An adjective clause, however, is not independent. It does not make sense by itself as an independent clause does; furthermore, it must always attach to an independent clause. The independent clause in this sentence is *A car drove by the house.*

Complex Sentences

Review adjectives on page 66 and adverbs on page 70.

There are two other kinds of dependent clauses—adverb and noun. They too serve the same functions as one-word adverbs and nouns respectively. Sentences which contain a dependent clause and an independent clause are called **complex** sentences.

The quickest way to identify dependent clauses is by the first word. Adjective clauses begin with a **relative pronoun** and adverb clauses with a **subordinating conjunction.** Noun clauses begin with words from a special group. Occasionally the first word of the clause may be understood—that is, it is not necessary to the sentence but could be used.

Where is the comb (that) you borrowed from me?

You should be able to tell from the structure of the clause (subject and predicate but no complete thought) that it is dependent with or without the introductory word.

Study the following summary of the dependent clauses. Then complete the exercises that follow.

Adjective Clauses modify nouns; begin with relative pronouns; answer question: *What kind of?*

relative pronouns

who	I asked the woman *who wrote the letter.*
whom	I asked the woman *to whom the letter pertained.*
whose	I asked the man *whose gloves I found.*
which	I painted the house *which my brother had bought.*
that	I selected the watch *(that) I wanted most.* (Understood)

Adverb Clauses modify verbs, adjectives, other adverbs; begin with subordinating conjunctions; answer questions: *how? when? where? to what extent or degree? why? under what conditions?*

Complex Sentences

subordinating conjunctions

after	so that
although	than
as	that
as if	though
as long as	unless
as soon as	until
because	when
before	whenever
if	where
in order that	wherever
since	while

When?   I ate lunch *after I had washed up.*

How?   I ate lunch *as if I were starved.*

Why?   I was alarmed *because you had missed the message.*

To what extent?   I thought you would come later *than we'd planned.*

Where?   *Wherever you go,* I will find you.

Noun Clauses   act like nouns; answer questions: *Who or what did it? what? whom?*

begin with

that	how
what	if (whether)
wherever	when
which	whether
who	why
whoever	whose

What? *Whatever you say* is okay.

What? He will like *whatever you say.*

Who? I will be *whoever you want me to be* in the play.

Whom? I will send *whoever wants one* a red balloon.

Write sentences that include these adjective clauses.

1. to whom he left a million
2. which was smoldering under the ashes
3. that I'd met on a picnic
4. who treats me like a child
5. whose salary is higher than mine
6. that has my hat
7. who knows the role of Violetta

Make up sentences that include these adverb clauses.

1. when I get my diploma
2. before he goes any further
3. wherever there is a bargain
4. while you are still young and capable
5. as long as they agree
6. before you leave
7. after the work is finished

Write sentences that use these noun clauses.

1. that the building would collapse
2. whose signature it was
3. if I can go or not
4. who won
5. whom you sent to him
6. whatever they decide
7. whoever understands French

Write one sentence for each of these pictures. Use an adjective clause, an adverb clause and a noun clause.

Complex Sentences

Write clauses at the carets in these sentences. Be sure the clause has subject and verb. Refer to the chart to see which words introduce each kind of dependent clause.

Adjective Clauses

1. The cabbie ∧ jerked to an abrupt stop.
2. He jumped out and took my suitcase ∧.
3. Aunt Mabel ∧ ran up to greet me.
4. We walked together through the airport ∧.
5. The agent ∧ assigned me a seat in the smoking section.

Adverb Clauses The subordinating conjunctions are supplied for you.

1. We arrived at the picnic after ∧
2. Since ∧, he was investigating job openings in carpentry.
3. Although ∧, they couldn't travel as they had dreamed they would.
4. You just wait until ∧
5. He is studying chemistry in order that ∧

Noun Clauses

1. Give this letter to ∧
2. I don't know ∧
3. Mrs. Grambley verbally attacked ∧
4. Jack realized ∧
5. The professor clearly understood ∧
6. The reason is ∧
7. The reason Gerry won the contest is ∧
8. I read in the newspaper ∧
9. I saw in a magazine ∧
10. ∧ is his most striking characteristic.

Even though a dependent clause has a subject and verb, it also has an introductory word that keeps it from making sense by itself. If a dependent clause is written as an independent element, beginning with a capital and ending with a period, it is a fragment.

Sentence Fragments 93

>   **no** Since aerosols are now thought to contribute to pollution. I never buy them.

Correct a fragment by constructing an independent clause to go with it or by joining the dependent clause to a nearby independent clause.

>   **yes** Since aerosols are now thought to contribute to pollution, I never buy them.
>
>   **or** Aerosols are now thought to contribute to pollution. For that reason, I never buy them.

Correct these sentences.

1. Memorial Day is a national holiday. Because we commemorate lives laid down in the cause of freedom.
2. July 4 is the memorial of the signing of the Declaration of Independence. Which took place in Philadelphia in 1776.
3. Labor Day provides a day off for workers and students at the beginning of September. Just before they begin the long winter's toil.
4. Thanksgiving, of course, celebrates the blessings of liberty and plenty. That were found by the Pilgrim settlers at Plymouth Rock.
5. New Year's Day, which is January 1. It is followed by Presidents' Day in February, another winter holiday.

Rewrite these sentences making them complex.

1. Shining moments enter into every life. They brim with beauty and shimmer with happiness.
2. They come at different times. You may be looking down a blazing autumn road or at a towering skyscraper.
3. You are walking distractedly down an ordinary avenue. A streetlight may for a magic moment appear as a star.
4. Your thoughts explode—free, light, bright. Before they were heavy and clotted as mud.
5. You would like to crystallize those moments. All the meaning of life is contained in them. You want them to last forever and ever.

One more type of sentence is the most involved of all. Called *compound-complex,* it has two independent clauses and one or more dependent clause which may be adjective, adverb or noun or all three.

                 dependent noun clause   First Ind. Cl. conj.
[That I had to wait by the lake for you] was lucky AND

  Second Ind. Cl.   dep. adv. clause   dependent adv. clause
I am grateful [because [while I waited] I was suddenly

                                       dep. adj. clause
inspired to write the poem] [that won the $100,000 prize.]

Identify the two independent clauses in each of these sentences as well as all the dependent clauses.

1. Some people confuse the Dutch game of *kolf* with the Scottish-originated golf, but the Dutch game bears no more resemblance to golf than a pinball machine.
2. For one thing, *kolf* is played in a *kolf-bann,* which is an indoor ice-rink about 100 × 25 feet; moreover, it follows rules that are very much like American hockey.
3. But the Scottish golf which derives from the Germanic word *kolbe* or *club,* dates back five and a half centuries and the Dutch Rembrandt etching of 1645 that is named "The Golfer" should really be called "The *Kolfer.*"
4. The Scottish King James II (1685) declared golf illegal because its popularity was interfering with the archery practice of the citizen army; this suggests that the game must have been in wide favor for many years.

Gerunds and Infinitives and Such

Gerunds and infinitives are two kinds of structures that function as nouns. They are called verbals because both derive from verbs and retain some of the properties of verbs; for example, they can take objects.

    A **gerund** is the *-ing* form of the verb with no auxiliary. You have already studied participles, verbals functioning like adjectives.

    Singing in the shower, Jo stubbed her toe.

Gerunds and Infinitives 95

You met participle phrases on page 73.

Singing in the shower is a participle phrase modifying the noun *Jo*. Compare the same phrase in this sentence.

Singing in the shower can be dangerous.

Here *singing in the shower* is a gerund, a verbal phrase acting as the subject of the sentence. It could also be the direct object of a transitive verb, or serve any other function a noun does.

Jo enjoys singing in the shower. (direct object of *enjoys*)

How is the same phrase different in this sentence?

Jo is singing in the shower.

If you have trouble with this verb, review page 63.

You should recognize that *singing* is the main verb of this sentence because the auxiliary *is* precedes it.

Find the gerunds in these sentences. Don't be misled by verbs with auxiliaries or by participles.

1. Fishing is his favorite recreation.
2. He is fishing for pike.
3. Fishing the stream, Albert fell in.
4. Knowing the law had saved her life.
5. The study of history requires understanding patterns.
6. Collecting the garbage and disposing of it are separate problems.
7. Riding the crest of the wave, Murph suddenly flipped.
8. Recognizing gerunds is not difficult.
9. To Lee, winning means everything.
10. They thanked us for helping.
11. Crossing the stream, the rabbits almost drowned.
12. She believes in recognizing one's limitations.
13. They are looking for a new home.
14. Realizing her mistake, Candace turned back.
15. Seeing is believing.

Gerunds and Infinitives

See page 57 for help with determiners.

Because they function as nouns, gerunds can sometimes be preceded by determiners. Don't make the mistake of using an object pronoun before a gerund. Use a possessive pronoun.

no Were you upset by me winning?

yes Were you upset by my winning?

What possessive pronoun would you use in each of these sentences?

1. ____ missing the spittoon annoyed the manager.
2. Do you like ____ playing?
3. ____ getting low grades may ruin my plans.
4. How does ____ refusing to take your son along affect your wife?
5. I admire ____ sticking to a project till she finishes it.

Infinitives are verbals that also function as nouns and sometimes as modifiers. They are formed with the preposition *to* plus the simple form of the verb, that is, the form with no inflections.

To win was his aim.   (subject of sentence)

He'd like **to win** the lottery.   (direct object of sentence with its own object, *the lottery*)

We searched for a chair **to refinish**.   (modifies *chair*)

Don't confuse infinitives with prepositional phrases introduced by *to*. Prepositional phrases always take a noun or pronoun as object; in an infinitive, a verb follows *to*.

Andy is going **to bed** now.   (prepositional phrase)

Her last chore is **to bed down the horses for the night**.
(infinitive phrase)

Identify all the infinitives in these sentences. Don't be confused by prepositional phrases.

We decided to take a trip to Florida to see Disneyland. We found we had to wait as long as an hour or more to get on the rides. To top it all off, the car to the left of us in the parking lot scratched our fender as it tried to pull out.

Consistency

For more on this, see page 203.

The biggest problem you face with gerunds and infinitives is being consistent when you use a series of verbals or clauses. If you begin with a gerund phrase, don't switch to some other form halfway through the sentence.

no Her hobbies are swimming, singing and *to ride*.

yes Her hobbies are swimming, singing and *riding*.

Make the forms in these sentences consistent.

1. During his lifetime, he took up painting, writing and he taught for a while.
2. Can you understand what anyone sees in tap dancing and to sing in a chorus?
3. Clicking a camera, setting a tape in motion and even to arrange slides for a visual presentation were the things he liked to do best.
4. For centuries people have enjoyed mountain climbing, cave exploration and just to explore open fields.
5. The newspaper prints patterns every day for people who like to crochet, to knit, to weave and that lost art, tatting.

Make up a consistent form to end each series in these sentences. If you don't know the real facts, make some up.

1. Every evening Sylvester's last actions were adjusting the thermostat, putting out the cat, locking the front door and _____.
2. Wilma liked to whistle when she went past dark cemeteries, to hum when she brought in the morning milk and _____.

3. Mary Todd Lincoln's greatest pleasure was shopping; Eleanor Roosevelt's, becoming involved; and Jacqueline Kennedy's, ____.

4. Before you begin to cook, it is wise to assemble your ingredients, to read the recipe several times, to have the pans you need ready, and ____.

PROBLEM AREAS

You remember that a participle is an *-ing* form of the verb that functions as an adjective. Sometimes writers mistake participles for verbs and participle phrases for sentences.

Adam slipped on a banana peel. Falling and breaking his leg.

Falling and breaking his leg has no subject. Even if it had one, as this sentence has,

Carl training his own band.

what word would be needed to make it a sentence? The auxiliary *is* can make this a complete sentence.

Carl *is* training his own band.

Every sentence needs a complete subject and verb. One way to eliminate *-ing* fragments is to join them with the sentence that precedes them.

Adam slipped on a banana peel, falling and breaking his leg.

Another way is to put an *-ing* phrase at the beginning of a sentence.

Slipping on a banana peel, Adam fell and broke his leg.

Knit these word groups into sentences with participle phrases.

1. Toulouse-Lautrec was a talented painter. Specializing in painting cafe society.

Sentence Fragments 99

2. Drawing thick black outlines in his pictures of religious subjects. Rouault was at first thought strange in his techniques.
3. A Dutchman, Van Gogh, painted in the blazing sun. Finally going mad and cutting off his own ear.
4. Creating impressions by the use of thousands of small dots. Seurat is a well-known impressionist.
5. Ballet is a favorite subject of Degas. Making space as well as line and color a part of his compositions.
6. Distorting his figures by elongating them. The Spanish artist El Greco painted mystic scenes.
7. Monet painted cathedrals hundreds of times. Thus hoping to show the different effects of light.
8. Showing several sides of a figure at once. Like Einstein in math, Picasso drew relativity.
9. Jackson Pollack's canvases look splotched. Dribbles of paint thrown down to create pleasing combinations.
10. Straight geometric forms were Mondrian's specialty. His paintings resembling large monopoly or chess boards with the blocks interestingly varied in size, shape and color.

Fragments

A phrase is not a sentence and cannot stand alone. When it is written that way, it is an error known as a *fragment*.

How would you correct these sentence fragments?

The men ran barefoot. Over the sand. (prepositional phrase)

The men ran. Singing exuberantly. (participle phrase)

I like ice cream. But not sherbet. (contrastive phrase)

Make the fragments part of the sentences in these.

1. A good diet may include any combination of fats and carbohydrates, but it must contain at least ten percent protein. As well as vitamins, minerals and water.
2. The Zen Macrobiotic Diet, which consists of large quantities of brown rice, is probably the most dangerous fad diet. Especially for expectant mothers.

100 Sentence Fragments

3. Vegetarian diets are least dangerous. Provided the vegetables chosen have adequate protein.
4. Potentially dangerous are fad diets that emphasize special foods to the exclusion of others. Like molasses, yogurt or honey.
5. Massive doses of vitamins, particularly A and D. Overdoses of the first can cause a rise in spinal fluid pressure. The second. It can even prove lethal.

Build tighter constructions by using a

1. (participle) Many students suddenly begin to study during their sophomore year. They see the need for good grades.
2. (infinitive) Mother puts cod liver oil in orange juice. It has a disagreeable taste.
3. (gerund) Don't start to eat before your hostess. It is bad manners.
4. (participle) Jerry was wearing his best suit. He planned to ask for a raise.
5. (gerund) I believe in this: to know what you want from life.

The paragraphs below contain fragments. Correct them by integrating the fragments into complete sentences. Keep the sense.

Handwriting is a human action that expresses the individuality of the writer. And is consistent with other expressions of personality. Movement to the left, such as back flourishes symbolize the past. Origin, mother and childhood. To the right, lies the work ahead. The future, the writer's life and social world. Tall letters show gravitation toward spiritual and intellectual phrases. Movements below symbolize descent into the material, subhuman and subconscious world. Handwriting can tell much about personality. But not age and sex.

Pressure is the degree of energy forced with the pen. Especially visible on the downstrokes. Symbolizing libido, Or state of health, vitality, will power and depth of feeling. Heavy pressure shows much energy in these areas. Lack of pressure shows the opposite. There are many pressures. Heavy, medium heavy, light, medium light, weak and light, uneven and wavering. Periodic, smeary, muddy and broken.

Heavy pressure. With large capitals. These show drive that easily becomes self-centered. With the individual stepping on others. Hoods on crossed *t*'s show aggressiveness. Interfering with full success. Uneven pressure. Is usually a sign of mental abnormality. Equal heaviness of pressure shows love of rich colors, soft fabrics. And closeness to nature, warmth and creativity.

Slant. In handwriting is the angle which the downstrokes form with the base line. It shows emotional makeup and relationship to past, present and future. There are three. Rightward. Which shows affection and social tenderness. The more the slant tends to the right, the less control there is over the emotions. And the greater the social interest. The vertical slant. Symbolizing poise and intellectual control. Maybe five degrees leftward or rightward of the 90-degree vertical. Left or backward slant. Is concern with one's ego. Loss of naturalness and some kind of artificiality. The further left the slant, the more the writer is removed from reality. Having dominating memories of past experiences.

People whose lines tilt up on a page are optimistic and cheerful. And ambitious. Concave lines show persons who begin a project in self-distrust, and having once begun, finish successfully. Downward writing, which you probably can guess. Reveals a trend toward melancholy, pessimism. And madness. Convex curves. These show zeal and ambition but not perseverance. Letters that are all connected. These show a logical mind, always thinking systematically and practically. Disconnected writing shows intuitiveness. Emotional sensitivity and originality. All letters disconnected. Show unsociableness, uncooperativeness. And jumping to conclusions.

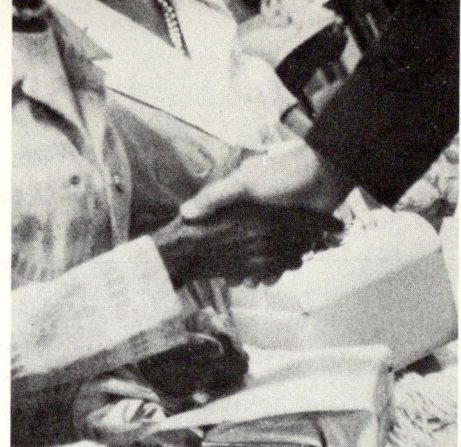

In Agreement

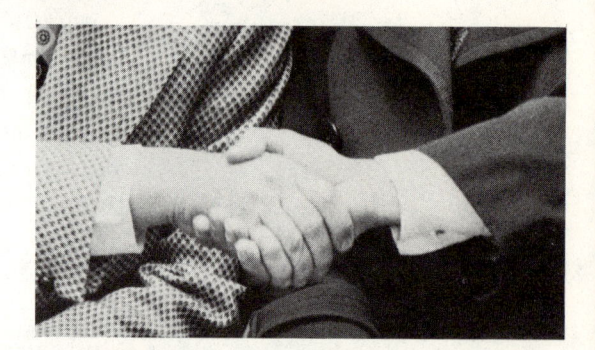

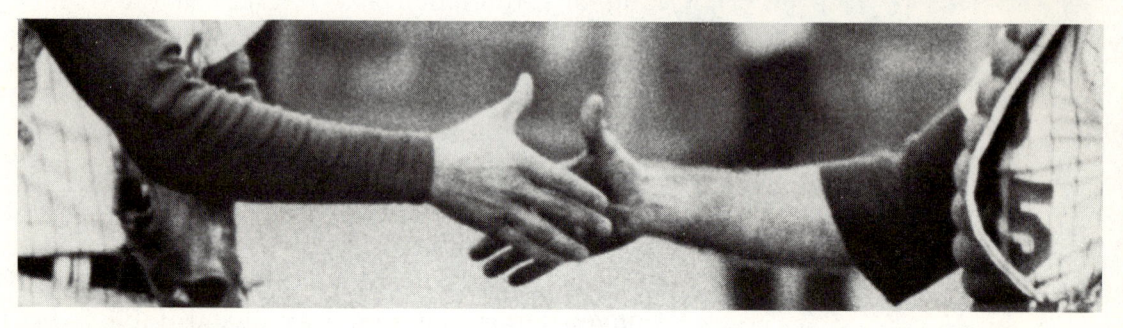

Everyone knows that a singular subject takes a singular verb,

>Corrine *grows* chives next to her roses to keep the aphids away.

and that a plural subject takes a plural verb.

>The *farmers say* that garlic will also keep aphids away.

But agreement is not always an easy matter. Some words can present problems.

Do you know which verbs are compatible with the subjects in these sentences?

C   **1.** The track team (run, runs) four miles every day.

Q   **2.** Twenty-five dollars (is, are) burning a hole in my pocket.

I   **3.** Each man, woman and child (is, are) responsible for the prevention of forest fires.

P   **4.** German measles (is, are) harmful to expectant mothers.

D   **5.** There (is, are) fifteen barrels of pickles down here.

S   **6.** Neither Bob nor Ethel (wants, want) to do the dishes.

W   **7.** Abe was one of those melancholy men who (thinks, think) much and (speaks, speak) little.

T   **8.** *Leaders and Followers* (is, are) one of the best books I've read.

F   **9.** One of my good alligator shoes (is, are) worn through.

Refer to the letter key before each sentence to find out why you missed the sentences you did.

S   Compound Subjects

When the subject of a sentence is compound, agreement of subject and verb sometimes presents a challenge.

1. Compound subjects joined by *and* always take plural verbs, no matter whether they occur before or after the verb.

> Fruits, vegetables, meal, milk and cereal **are** the basics of solid nutrition.

> Below the ground **were** a secret tunnel and a doorway leading to freedom.

> Both blackbird and bluejay **have** annoying squawks.

2. Compound subjects that express a single idea take singular verbs.

> Ham and eggs **is** my favorite breakfast. (one dish)

> His wife and sweetheart from childhood **watches** at his bedside. (one person)

3. When a compound subject is joined by *or* or *nor*, the verb is singular.

   Greg **or** Ernie **walks** the dog. (Either one does.)

4. When a singular and a plural subject are joined by *or, nor, either, neither* or *nor*, the verb agrees with the subject nearer the verb.

   The children **or** their **father shops** every day.

   The father **or** the **children shop** every day.

   Neither Tim **nor** his **brothers sing** in the choir.

   Neither the boys **nor Anita sings** in the choir.

5. When a whole compound subject is modified by *each, every, neither* or *no*, use a singular verb.

   Every market, bazaar and stall in India **was** flooded with people.

In each sentence supply the compatible verb. Then reverse the order of the subjects and supply the right verb form.

come   1. The dolphin or the seals _____ up periodically for food.

make   2. Either the seals or the dolphins _____ a big show flipping and squawking.

refuse   3. Neither the average adult nor the children ever _____ them fish.

be   4. Herrings or a big fat sardine _____ the usual bait for the show.

reject   5. Neither the dolphin nor the seals ever _____ the prized reward.

know   6. Neither the dolphin nor the seals _____ when to say no to food.

set   7. Either the zoo keepers or the zoo director _____ a limit on how much they are fed.

be   8. A zoo director or other executives _____ expected to know their capacity.

make   9. Because either the zoo owner or the stockholders of the animals _____ money on the show, fish sales are carefully controlled.

be   10. But neither the sardine man nor the sellers of herring _____ happy about the arrangement.

Subject-Verb Agreement

Notice that, when there is a verb phrase, the subject agrees with the auxiliary, not the main verb.

Decide whether the verb should be singular or plural.

1. Music, ballet and theater (fills, fill) her spare moments.
2. The cat or the dog (is, are) making this mess.
3. Forming an eerie background for the cemetery (is, are) rows of twisted trees.
4. Neither Betsy nor her cousins (plans, plan) to go.
5. Whitcomb, Miller, Fenner and Smith (is, are) broadcasting the stock market reports.
6. Neither Mick nor his opponents (is, are) in favor of holding the fight here.
7. Tom or Bob (is, are) responsible for the disorder.
8. The missile will have a deeper thrust than any other so far (says, say) the authorities.
9. Each filly and mare (was, were) branded.
10. Either you or I (am, are) to get the award.
11. My friend and neighbor Roberts (is, are) a construction worker.
12. Either you or your friends always (finds, find) the right solution.
13. His mother says that weiners and beans (has, have) always been his favorite dish.
14. They reported that not only Jim but all the men on board (was, were) also stricken by the strange disease.
15. Clare, Cathy and Claudia each (wants, want) her own bedroom.

Write original sentences with each kind of compound subject you just practiced. Start the first sentence with "macaroni and cheese . . ."

I Indefinite Numbers

Indefinite pronouns are the trickiest agreement problem. Whether the indefinite is the subject of a sentence or a determiner before the subject, follow these rules.

1. Clearly singular: *each, every, either, neither, another, anyone, anything, someone, no one* and, especially in writing, *anybody, everybody, somebody, anyone,* and *everyone.*

    Each is responsible for one book.

2. Clearly plural: *both, few, many, several.*

    Both enjoy a good movie.

3. Singular or plural according to sense: *all, any, none, some, most, the rest, a part, half, two-thirds.* When these expressions indicate *how many* and indicate something you can count, use a *plural* verb:

    Half the pickles **were** moldy.

    When they indicate *how much,* use a *singular* verb:

    Half the roast **was** eaten.

Choose the standard English form.

1. Each girl (is, are) expected to wear a bathing cap.
2. Every dog (is, are) carefully checked for fleas.
3. I don't know if either (is, are) going.
4. (Is, Are) another carload coming?
5. Both men (is, are) coming.
6. Many children (experiences, experience) hunger.
7. Several of the lights (is, are) burned out.
8. All the world (know, knows) who did it.
9. Only half the upstairs (is, are) cleaned.
10. (Is, Are) some of the candy left?
11. (Is, Are) some of the peppermint candies left?
12. None of the problems (is, are) correct.
13. Everybody here (take, takes) sugar.
14. Each of us (want, wants) better housing for the poor.
15. Neither of them (cares, care) for chocolate.

Certain unusual phrases will give you no problem if you follow these simple rules.

many a singular: *Many a* child *has* asked Santa for a toy.

a number of plural: *A number* of people *are* here.

the number singular: *The number* of people here *is* small.

kind, type, sort singular: The *kind* of pie you want *isn't* available.

kinds, types, sorts plural: What *kinds* of shoes are your favorites?

Write a sentence for each item below following the directions exactly. Be imaginative.

1. Tell about the kinds of singing groups you enjoy most, use the word *kinds*.
2. Refer to *the number* of dogs in your neighborhood in a sentence.
3. Cite some of your favorite courses; tell in a few sentences, in which you use *a number of*, about some of them.
4. Using *many a* make a generalization about sports participation.
5. Use the phrase *kind of* in sentences discussing current headgear in your locality.

C Collective Nouns

Some words that appear singular may be plural and take a plural verb. Words that are singular in form but that name groups of persons or things are known as *collective* nouns.

army	club	crowd	jury	public
audience	committee	family	mob	squad
chorus	couple	group	nation	team
class	crew	herd	pair	troop

Collective nouns can be either singular or plural. When you refer to the group acting as a unit, use a singular verb.

The **crew was** one hundred percent behind the captain.

When you refer to the individual parts or members of the group acting separately, use a plural verb.

The **crew were** divided about the mutiny.

Hint: If a pronoun following the verb is singular, the verb should be singular; if it is plural, the verb should be plural.

The squad has named **its** leader.

The squad have made up **their** minds to win.

Which verb is correct?

1. The couple (is, are) considering buying a house.
2. That family (has, have) their ups and down.
3. The army (is, are) sending its best men to the front.
4. The male chorus (practices, practice) their various voice parts on different nights.
5. The team (is, are) determined to make their quota of $2,000.

Write two sentences: the first should regard this group as a unit, the second, as individuals.

P Plural Words

Certain nouns ending in *-s* or *-ics* that name diseases or a body of knowledge are singular and take a singular verb: *measles, mumps, physics, mathematics, economics, civics, politics,* and *news.*

Measles makes the rounds every spring.

Physics is a challenging subject.

What **news is** he spreading?

Use the plural verb for *pants, suspenders, scissors, tweezers,* etc., unless you are saying "a pair of."

The **scissors are** on the table.

A **pair of scissors is** on the table.

Write the correct form of the verb.

be	1. ____ the scissors in the drawer?
be	2. Your suspenders ____ broken.
do	3. Mathematics ____ his mind a world of good.
be	4. Linguistics ____ the science of language.
be	5. The intricate dynamics of the moonshot ____ understood by very few.
be	6. The news ____ all good.
get	7. Politics ____ into your blood.
be	8. ____ there a pair of trousers in the closet?
reveal	9. Statistics ____ that birth rates in the U.S. are on a decline.
be	10. The tweezers ____ on the table.

Beginning "I think ____ is," write a sentence describing any of the subjects on the list of plural words.

T Titles

Titles of books, articles, plays, etc., take singular verbs.

    "Jack and the Beanstalk" **is** a story every child should read.

Choose the correct verb.

1. *The Side Streets of New York* (is, are) one of the books I read last week.
2. *The Hidden Persuaders* (is, are) a book that reveals the machinations of advertising.
3. *Flowers and Flowering Bushes* (sell, sells) for $10.95.

Using the name of a book you've read recently as the first word, write a sentence.

Q Quantities

When plural nouns of measure, figures or money express a single unit, use a singular verb.

    Ten **dollars is**n't much these days.

    I said three **inches is** too wide a hem.

Which verb is correct?

1. His three hundred pounds (make, makes) buying clothes a problem.
2. (Is, Are) a hundred dollars too much to ask?
3. Fourteen gallons (costs, cost) $7.38.
4. Seven times eight (is, are) fifty-six.
5. Your five cents (is, are) under the dresser.

Write a sentence telling how much money you have with you today (or the last time you went shopping). Put the amount first.

Review all the rules.

1. (Is, Are) your fifteen dollars safe here?
2. A number of people (likes, like) late movies.

3. Two-thirds of the laundry (was, were) received.
4. *Jaws* (is, are) a good book to start with.
5. Half the committee (isn't, aren't) here.
6. The committee (disagree, disagrees) among themselves.
7. Each (wants, want) a new bathing suit.
8. The news (is, are) spreading like wildfire.
9. Athletics (take, takes) a great deal of his time.
10. *The New York Times* (circulate, circulates) half a million copies daily.
11. That class (has, have) always wanted its own way.
12. The jury (was, were) unanimous in their decision to acquit him.
13. Exactly two cents (is, are) left in my wallet.
14. *The Merry Wives of Windsor* (is, are) one of Shakespeare's comedies.
15. The scissors (was, were) rusty.
16. The mechanics of refrigeration (isn't, aren't) complex.
17. Everyone (is, are) welcome.
18. Half the horse barns (was, were) lit before dawn.

D Dummy Subjects

Sentence constructions such as the two dummy subjects *there* and *it*, can make subject-verb agreement confusing. A *be* verb introduced by *there* or *it* agrees with the subject following it.

> There *is* one *motorcycle* in the lab.

> There *are* ten dune *buggies* here.

W Relative Clauses

The verb in a relative clause always agrees with the subject of the clause. If the subject of the clause is a pronoun, the word it refers to determines the number of the verb.

>   **pl.**   **pl.**
> It is the children **who** are making all the noise.

Ignore any dummy subjects in these sentences to make subject and verb agree.

1. There (is, are) many kinds of cancer.
2. (There was, were) no room in the hotel.
3. It is people who (loves, love) life that (spread, spreads) joy.
4. It is the last two hours that (seems, seem) the longest.
5. There (is, are) a good many people who (advocates, advocate) change.

F   Intervening Phrase

The verb agrees with the subject even when a phrase that seems to make it plural comes between.

One (of the girls) **is** dressing now.

Make the subjects and verbs agree in these sentences.

1. Migration to the cities (has, have) left the inner cities to the poor.
2. Each of the animals (was, were) fleeing before the fire.
3. Jerry, one of my closest acquaintances, (call, calls) me every night.
4. One of the members of the committee (wants, want) more time.
5. Alec, with braces on his teeth and stars in his eyes, (wants, want) a new car.
6. The only one of her books I liked (was, were) the last.
7. The Ohio is one of the rivers that (flows, flow) into the Misssissippi.
8. One of the authors (has, have) written about the Bermuda triangle.

Choose the correct verb for each sentence.

1. Most of the building (was, were) ransacked.
2. If either of you (wins, win), I hope you will remember me.
3. Mathematics (is, are) a difficult course for my cousin.
4. You or Betty (was, were) mentioned for the position.
5. The Navy (needs, need) men like you.

6. Mary or Glen usually (mows, mow) that side of the lawn.
7. Art, history and literature (combines, combine) to reveal culture.
8. A lick and a promise (is, are) all she had time for.
9. There (isn't, aren't) any soap left.
10. The principal, as well as the supervisors, (was, were) concerned.
11. When economics (is, are) abolished from the curriculum, I will cheer.
12. Fish and chips (is, are) a dish I love.
13. The chipmunk or the squirrels (is, are) responsible for those tunnels.
14. There (is, are) not many people who dance as well as Milly.
15. *Numbers* (is, are) the fourth book of the Bible.
16. (Do, Does) no one want strawberry?
17. The Ohio Public Library network is one of the systems that (is, are) supported by intangible taxes.
18. Among the last to arrive (was, were) Angela and Carmella.
19. Every desk and chair in the library (is, are) being refinished.
20. Beyond the driveway and a little past the shed (run, runs) a shallow creek.

There are no agreement problems when you use the simple past tense.

Write an indefinite pronoun to fill the blank and a verb phrase to complete the sentence. Do not use the simple past tense.

    Example: __1__ of the windows VP

        Each of the windows was broken by a separate blast.

1. __1__ child or its mother VP
2. __1__ of the firemen VP
3. __1__ hop, skip and jump VP
4. __1__ the animals in the neighborhood VP

Make these subjects and verbs agree.

1. Fifteen newspapers (was, were) left lying in the rain.
2. The membership (has, have) decided to go their separate ways.

3. Each dog and each cat (want, wants) constant attention.
4. Linden & Taylors (sells, sell) quality furs.
5. Did you know that neither Gert nor her sisters (knows, know) how to skate?
6. For sale tomorrow (is, are) sports clothes and sporting goods.
7. Roberta, as well as Paula and Gene, (sings, sing) in the choir.
8. Twenty gallons of gas (is, are) the capacity of the tank.
9. The orchestra (practices, practice) their parts every day in different areas of the conservatory.
10. Half the school (is, are) absent today.
11. Ellie is one of those people who (exercises, exercise) daily.
12. Either candidate (is, are) counting on a sure win.
13. Pork and beans (is, are) improved by a little molasses.
14. I'm sorry, but thirty-five cents (is, are) all I have left.
15. The three-day measles (is, are) extremely contagious.

PRONOUN PROFICIENCY

You will see, as you work with this section, that many of the same problems are involved with pronoun agreement as with verb agreement.

What possessive pronoun would you place in the slot? His? His or her? Their?

Everybody should replace _____ own chair.

If you chose *their,* you are rolling with the punches. The antecedent of a pronoun is the noun or other pronoun to which it refers. In this case, the antecedent pronoun, *everybody,* is singular. In daily informal conversation, *their* is becoming acceptable when the antecedent is singular, but in writing, *their* is still frowned on. If you chose *his,* you probably understand pronoun agreement, but many people object to the use of a masculine pronoun when the antecedent is not necessarily masculine. If you wrote *his or her,* you show that you are up to date, but your ear for language rhythms leaves something to be desired.

What's the answer? Although pronoun usage is in a state of change, standard written usage requires that pronouns agree with their antecedents in gender and number. Gender is masculine and feminine. Number refers to singular or plural.

Marion wiped *her* glasses.

No problem. *Marion* is feminine and singular, as is *her*.

The *boys* sent *their* names to the press.

Again the case is clear. Both *boys* and *their* are plural and though *boys* is masculine, *their* is sexless. For the original sentence of this section, perhaps reconstruction is the only way out.

All *persons* should replace *their* chairs.

More serious problems arise when certain classes of nouns and pronouns are antecedents. The indefinite pronouns present the greatest challenge.

Certain pronouns are always singular: *each, every, either, neither, one, no one, nobody* and, at least in written English, *anyone, anybody, everyone, someone, somebody.*

Each wanted **his** own way.

That's simple enough. But these pronouns often appear with prepositional phrases that introduce a plural word between the pronoun and its antecedent.

Each of the men here wants the best for (his, their) family.

Because *men* is plural, you may be tempted to forget that *each*, a singular pronoun, is still the antecedent of the second pronoun. *His* is the correct choice to refer to *each: Each . . .* wants the best for *his* family.

Write the subject and the correct pronoun form for each sentence. Determine whether these sentences have prepositional phrases that may cause confusion.

1. No one wants (his, their) children to die.
2. Everyone of the marines was expected to keep (his, their) cool.
3. Neither of the bears was in (his, their) den.
4. Everybody should mind (his, their) own business.

5. Somebody wants (his, their) picture taken.
6. Where can anyone sharpen (her, their) pencil in these offices?
7. Each of the flowers (blooms, bloom) at a different time.
8. Everybody, including the maintenance men, (is, are) invited.
9. Either will eat (his, their) dinner if you coax (him, them).
10. Does either of your sisters like (her, their) steak rare?
11. Everyone of the speakers referred to (his, their) notes.
12. Won't anyone of you donate (his, their) services next week?
13. Every man enjoys (his, their) dog.
14. No one of you would want (his, their) house destroyed.
15. Everybody in this country has a right to cast (his, their) vote.

Long-range Influence

When singular indefinite pronouns modify compound subjects, the second pronoun is singular.

> **Every** table, lamp and chair was moved in order to accent **its** best qualities.

Choose the right form for these pronouns with long-range influence.

1. Every policeman and sanitation worker wanted (his, their) pay raised.
2. Each student, teacher, and administrator in the school showed (his, their) loyalty to the country.
3. Neither of the stewardesses would do anything to jeopardize (her, their) passengers' lives.

Some pronouns are always plural: *both, few, many, several.*

> **Both** wanted **their** own way.

These pronouns are either singular or plural, depending on the meaning intended: *all, some, any, none, most.*

All of the equipment was at **its** peak performance. (Treated as one unit.)

All of the rangers were at **their** posts. (Treated as separate units.)

Choose the singular or plural pronoun for each sentence.

1. Few of those present want to leave (his, their) children alone.
2. Many of the turkeys were losing (his, their) feathers.
3. After the flood, all the land changed (its, their) face.
4. None of the trees had (its, their) roots pulled out.
5. Several of the TV repairmen prefer to take (his, their) vacation now.
6. Adrienne's cake was popular because of (its, their) custard filling.
7. Most of the oranges were mushy right at (its, their) blossom end.
8. Some of the flowers were missing (its, their) leaves.

A few pronouns are in a state of change: *anyone, anybody, someone, somebody, everybody, everyone.* The following sentences might be acceptable for casual conversation, but standard written English requires the traditional form. Supply it.

1. Everybody took their seats.
2. Does anyone want their windows washed?
3. Everybody loves their parents, don't they?
4. Somebody left their gloves in the bus.
5. Anybody can have their palm read free.

Write one sentence with each type of indefinite pronoun.

Avoid one other problem with correlative conjunctions by consulting page 204.

Correlatives

Two or more singular antecedents joined by *or-nor* or *neither-nor* should be referred to by a singular pronoun.

Neither Donna **nor** Georgia brought **her** purse.

Demonstrative pronouns *this* and *that* agree with the word they modify. *This* and *that* are singular. *These* and *those* are plural.

This kind of work   **These kinds** of people

That kind of work   **These kinds** of shoes

Choose the correct pronoun for each sentence.

1. Either Mickey or Joe broke (his, their) fingers.
2. I don't care for (this, these) kinds of parties.
3. (That, Those) three kinds of pollen irritate my eyes.
4. Neither of the brothers told (his, their) story straight.
5. In the panic, either Irene or Isabel dropped (her, their) wallet.
6. (This, These) kinds of boxes are hard to carry.
7. Do you enjoy (this, these) kind of pear?
8. Neither Ricardo nor his companion expected to see (his, their) family again.
9. (That, Those) sort of vacation suits me fine.
10. Either a lion or a jaguar caught (its, their) foot in the trap.

Write a sentence using this picture to help you express an either-or or neither-nor relationship.

Group Nouns

Collective nouns may be referred to by either a singular or plural pronoun depending on the meaning.

> The **committee** took **their** seats. (Treated as individuals)
>
> The **committee** submitted **its** report. (Treated as one unit)

Determine the sense of these.

1. The chess club played (its, their) individual games well.
2. That family wants to ship (its, their) furniture south.
3. The team are ready to personally declare allegiance to (its, their) coach.
4. The crowd were frenzied in (its, their) outcries.
5. The audience left en masse expressing (its, their) anger.

Relative Pronouns

Who and *whom* cause more confusion than any other relative pronouns. Standard written English requires *who* in subject or predicate nominative positions and *whom* in objective cases.

>   S
> **Who** are you?
>
> PN
> **Who** do you think you are?   (You do think you are *who*.)
>
>   S
> Betsy is the woman [**who** made the flag.]
>
>   S
> Gretchen is the girl [**who** (I think) won.] Disregard clauses that cut in.
>
>   OP   OP
> To **whom** did you send the letter? or **Whom** did you send the letter to?
>
>   O   S
> She is a person [**whom** everyone should know.] (Everyone should know **whom**.)

Helpful hints: If the pronoun comes before a verb, *who* will usually be correct. If it comes after a preposition, it should be *whom*. If it comes before a noun or pronoun, it should be *whom*. If a clause such as *I believe* or *I think* intervenes, disregard it and look at the first word after it. Follow these patterns.

    WHO verb   preposition WHOM   WHOM noun or pronoun

    WHO (I believe) verb   WHOM (I think) noun or pronoun

Supply the correct forms.

1. ____ are
2. ____ is
3. ____ will
4. ____ knows
5. ____ can

1. ____ are you?
2. ____ is my neighbor?
3. ____ will do the dishes?
4. ____ knows the answer?
5. ____ can help with the ironing?

1. to ____
2. for ____
3. by ____
4. in ____
5. under ____

1. To ____ did you give my keys?
2. For ____ did he write that song?
3. I don't know by ____ it was written.
4. He is an expert in ____ I have great trust.
5. Under ____ do you work?

1. That is a person ____ I know well.
2. She is the lady ____ you met last week.
3. Where is that cousin ____ he bragged about?
4. This is the minister ____ Jerry told you about.
5. He is a friend ____ anyone can admire.

1. Jeb is an acquaintance ____ knows me from way back.
2. Mr. White is the teacher ____ taught me all I know.
3. I know a conductor of an orchestra ____ gyrates wildly.
4. Where is the librarian ____ can find anything you need?
5. This is one doctor ____ needs a rest.

1. Janet is a leader ____ I think would make a good president.
2. Barb is an artist ____ I believe will make it.

3. This boy is a worker ____ I know you will find diligent.
4. Here is a preacher ____ I'm sure they will accept.
5. Sonny is a singer ____ we all know has a good future.

Choose *who, whom, whoever, whomever* **for each sentence. (***Whoever*** fits into the same slots as** *who;* ***whomever,*** **into the same as** *whom.***)**

1. Mom, ____ called last night?
2. Give the package to ____ comes to the door.
3. The padded cell was built for anyone ____ needs it.
4. Tell ____ answers the phone that I'm out.
5. I'll give this gift to ____ I choose.
6. Isn't that the salesman ____ you threw out yesterday?
7. Why aren't there more dentists ____ don't make you wait?
8. Are these the people ____ you said Dennis wants to pay?
9. They are the ones ____ I suppose he was talking about.
10. Jackie is the kind of girl ____ I think might take the responsibility.

Write one sentence with each of the four forms of *who* **using this picture for inspiration.**

Review your pronoun proficiency.

1. Leslie is one person (who, whom) I believe will make a fine doctor.
2. (Who, whom) told you to come?
3. The jury are divided in (its, their) thinking.
4. Those (kind, kinds) of stories scare me.
5. Neither June nor Melanie (plan, plans) to attend college.
6. No one of the hikers is thinking of bringing (his, their) dog.
7. Each dog and each cat must wear (its, their) collar.
8. Every one of the members of the woman's guild needs help on (her, their) project.
9. Someone in the party was snapping (his, their) gum noisily.
10. Either of the boys does (his, their) work well.
11. Neither person wants to admit (his, their) guilt.
12. Many expressed (their, his) regret.
13. Some of the vendors were destroyed by the injunction to get (his, their) flowers off the sidewalks.
14. Most of the bread had food coloring added to (its, their) batter.
15. Everybody wants (his, their) rights protected.
16. Either Beth or Nora charges for (their, her) paintings.
17. These (kind, kinds) of assignments drive me up a wall.
18. Charlie Brown's team members are protesting (its, their) rights.
19. To (who, whom) does that article refer?
20. (Who, Whom) do you think Bert is going to marry?

Make these subjects and verbs agree.

1. Only when all the votes (is, are) in, will he relax.
2. One of the men (was, were) sent from Washington.
3. My cousin and roommate Nelson (has, have) a new stereo.
4. This is one of the three courses that (contributes, contribute) to everyone's downfall.
5. There is one of the concourses that (leads, lead) into the field.
6. It is hopeful people who (changes, change) the world.
7. The number of women in the class (is, are) small.

8. Several cases of wine (was, were) emptied that winter.
9. Bob, together with Norm and us, (was, were) late.
10. A quart and a half of oil (is, are) all that this car takes.
11. Thongs, leather boots, sandals, clogs and sturdy shoes (lines, line) the floor of her closet.
12. Either Delores or her sister-in-law (needs, need) time away after Al's illness.
13. Mr. White the artist and cartoonist (gives, give) lessons at night.
14. (Isn't, aren't) twenty pounds a lot to lose at once?
15. Anyone (is, are) allowed in free.

Make a choice for each of these sentences.

1. The crew (practice, practices) on the river every day.
2. In the back of the cellar (was, were) an old rocking chair and a crib.
3. Ethel or Ray (take, takes) charge of Thanksgiving dinner.
4. Every sailboat, yacht, rowboat and raft in England (was, were) used in the evacuation.
5. My sister and best friend (is, are) always there when I need her.
6. Everyone in the class (has, have) done the assignment.
7. Neither Sandra nor Samantha (enjoy, enjoys) gardening.
8. When the chorus (vote, votes), they seldom agree.
9. Your trousers (is, are) too long.
10. She said that five dollars (is, are) all we can ask.
11. There (is, are) only two doughnuts left.
12. No one has finished (his, their) dinner.
13. Each of the women gave (her, their) opinion.
14. All of the men in the choir have received (his, their) music.
15. Neither Ralph nor Angelo will tell (his, their) age.
16. There is a man (who, whom) everyone admires.
17. Bailey is a teacher (who, whom) we all love.
18. I want to know (who, whom) took the apples.

CAPITALIZATION

Archy, a literary cockroach, was the invention of Don Marquis. Since he had to jump from key to key on the typewriter, he could not use capital letters. Fortunately, that is not your problem; learning to use capitals in the right places can be a problem, however. This chapter will help you overcome that handicap.

PFUI

don t you ever eat any sandwiches in your office
i haven t had a crumb of bread for i don t know how long
or a piece of ham or anything but apple parings
and paste leave a piece of paper in your machine
every night you can call me archy

PASTE

From the book *The Lives and Times of Archy and Mahitabel* by Don Marquis. Copyright 1928, 1932, 1935 by Don Marquis. Reprinted by permission of Doubleday & Co., Inc.

Capitalization: First Words

Capitalize the first word of every complete sentence. | The greatest oak was once a little nut that held its ground.

The first word of every quoted complete sentence is also capitalized but not a sentence fragment.

A great man once said, "**E**very noble work is at first impossible."

Tina called the incident "**a** big blooper."

The first word of a complete sentence following a colon is also capitalized.

The Judge made this pronouncement: **W**hereas the jury has found you not guilty, all charges are hereby declared void.

Capitalize the first word of each line of traditional poetry. | **S**he walks in beauty, like the night
Of cloudless climes and starry skies;

If you are writing in a narrow space, indent the runover line, but do not capitalize it.

She walks in beauty,
  like the night

Capitalize the first word of the salutation and complimentary close of a letter. | **D**ear old friend,
Very truly yours,

Try your wings. Write the words that should be capitalized.

1. the writer ended with the mysterious statement, "sentences are like worms."
2. the tension between the two countries is at breaking point. the assassination definitely complicated the issues. we sit in fear of the outcome of the new attempts at settlement.

3. his imagination plagued him with one question: how will this decision stand up in five years?
4. the *Times* named him "one of the richest men on earth."

Write any words that should be capitalized.

1. our renowned guest has written compositions in three forms: sonatas, concertos and fugues.
2. several things are necessary for good health; proper rest, adequate nutrition and sufficient exercise.
3. the president alerted the nation, saying, "we must cut back."
4. one vegetable I despise above every other: squash.
5. I beg you to consider the alternative: if she is acquitted, our children will again be in peril.
6. turning sharply on his little brother, he had only one thing to say, "scram."
7. your failure to respond will result in three tragedies: the world will be scandalized, the nation will be demoralized and lives will be wasted.
8. over and over again the problem revolved in his mind: where will I get the money?

Accent Proper Nouns

Common nouns identify classes of people or things: *men.* Proper nouns name particular things: *Tom, Dick, Harry.*

Capitalization: Proper Nouns 127

If the noun below is particular, make it common. If it is common, make it particular.

state	surgeon	mountain	hawthorne street
germany	ms. morris	pen	historical era
radio	julius	car	book
the bear barrel polka	shortie guggenbiller	johann sebastian bach	coach mccartney

Capitalize all proper nouns.
- **names of persons:** John Frederich McPherson, Tiny Sawicki
- **names of particular places:** Atlantic Ocean, Bloomington, Indiana, Webster Avenue
- **names of buildings:** Statler-Hilton Hotel

Capitalize the names of geographical areas, but not north, south, east and west when referring to directions.

the South   the Orient

We turned south on Green Street.

Write all words that should be capitalized.

1. When we visited the west, I was surprised at the loveliness of cactus blooms.
2. You will ride right into the heart of the western reserve by traveling 100 miles on route 71.
3. The economy of the south was heavily damaged by the Civil War.
4. You will find the wester medical building on the west corner of the intersection of monroe and east seventy-first street, ten minutes after you turn south at the junction of east hinterland drive and cooper-foster road.
5. Their vacation along the eastern seaboard included stops at virginia beach, atlantic city, fire island national seashore, block island, cape cod and acadia national park.

Capitalization: Proper Nouns

Prepare these addresses for mailing.

1. ms. jackie davies, 2649 east boulevard n. w., roanoke, va.
2. mr. garrett garrett, the osborne building, 1729 park court at westchester avenue, berlin, ohio
3. mr. and mrs. wendal benchley, 300 longshore drive, winona, minnesota
4. ms. thelma winston, 1479 thruman avenue, montgomery, alabama
5. dr. oscar weingard, c/o university hospital, 8 sixth street, tacoma, washington

Correctly capitalize the following.

1. cuyahoga county
2. the orient
3. robert moses state park
4. john macnulty
5. a town like amherst
6. the yukon in canada
7. glen canyon lake
8. westchester county
9. council bluffs, iowa
10. morrison-delaney parkway
11. the indian ocean
12. southern asia
13. san fernando valley
14. lake okeechobee
15. pecos river
16. petrified forest mountain park
17. mount rainier
18. central park, manhattan
19. chrysler building
20. detroit-superior bridge

Capitalize the names of particular things.

calendar events: Wednesday, February, Valentine's Day

but not seasons: spring, fall

peoples, languages, races, nationalities: Bantus, French, Caucasian, Czechoslovak

but not: blacks, whites

important words in the titles of **organizations, firms, schools:** National Wildlife Institute, Society for the Prevention of Cruelty to Animals, Prudential Life Insurance Corporation, Linton High School

courses: Health II, Writing for the Media

but not subjects: home economics, math

> **religions, orders, sects:** Protestant, Sister of St. Francis
>
> **services, prayers, sacred books:** Baptist, Mass, Our Father, Torah
>
> **documents, governing bodies:** Declaration of Human Rights, Supreme Court
>
> **political parties:** Republicans
>
> **vehicles:** Italia, Boeing 747, Datsun, Apollo 13
>
> **heavenly bodies:** Jupiter, Aquarius
>
>   *but not:* earth, moon, sun
>
> **eras, historical events, periods:** Gay Nineties, World War II, Victorian Age
>
> **trade names:** Heinz catsup

Capitalize the following as needed.

1. a sleek plymouth
2. renaissance period
3. ford foundation
4. league of nations
5. potsdam agreement
6. souped-up ford torino
7. andromeda (constellation)
8. centauri (star)
9. age of aquarius
10. diederick nursery
11. milky way
12. sirius (star)
13. december day
14. labor day

Write all the words that should be capitalized and make small all the words that are now capital and should not be.

    Educational Institutions often do not meet the needs of the average person. For instance, many people are interested in such practical subjects as Gardening, Photography, Simple Agriculture, Rocks, Fish, Geology, Animals, Modern Music and Archery. Others would like to take courses in such areas as The Psychic, Antiques, Sky Diving, Skin Diving, Coins and Stamps and even in How to Plan for the Future.

    In the large School, at most, all that are offered every other year are such courses as Photography I, Photography II and

Oceanography I. The first can be taken only by students in a program of Chemistry; the second only with an Earth Science program.

Capitalize personal titles used with a proper name.	**Mr.** & **Mrs.** Dean, **G**overnor Andrew Parker, Eleanor Wilson, **Ph.D.**, **O**ld Hickory, **P**resident of the U.S., **V**ice-president Rockefeller
Capitalize words showing family relationships when used as a name.	**A**unt Mildred, **G**randma Moses. Tell **D**ad I'm coming. *but not with a possessive:* His dad will pick you up at eight.
Capitalize the first, last and all important words of publications and works of art.	**A**lice in **W**onderland, the *Miami Herald*, "**T**he **P**it and the **P**endulum," "**L**ong **D**ay's **J**ourney into **N**ight," "**S**wan **L**ake," **M**ona **L**isa

Which words should be capitalized?

1. eugene kennedy, principal
2. the class president
3. president smith
4. andrea ashyk, d.d.s.
5. uncle eugene
6. the house of seven gables
7. mark spitz
8. judge benesh
9. my grandfather
10. a mormon

Capitalize the words that require it in these sentences.

1. on his tour of the west, principal darrell jackson collected slides to be used in photography II.
2. he also made them available to english and geography classes.
3. a harvard graduate and a staunch republican, mr. jackson received his m.s. in archaeology from western reserve university and then taught courses in ancient cultures in peoria, illinois.
4. as an assistant principal, he published "the worship of gold in cajamarca" for *the archaeologist* as well as a book, *gold rush in the inca empire,* for which he received a rave review in the *new york times.*

5. after a winter tour of pan-america he accepted the principalship of bradley secondary where he quickly mobilized the p.t.a., the boosters club and community resources "to cooperate in building an institution that will provide a rich horizon as well as in-depth education for the youth of this area."

Review: Capitalization.

1. do you attend st. stans church or b'nai abraham temple?
2. the freshmen and seniors are having a party.
3. the armies of the world are mobilizing.
4. do you think vassar will take him?
5. where is coach smith?
6. mr. smith is one of the coaches.
7. welcome, senator, to our meeting. george, take the senator down.
8. but lady, that's my hat!
9. the president spoke today. he asked americans to bite the bullet.
10. send it to the honorable j. f. bryne.
11. stay out of ellen's room! she's reading *alive!*
12. you can't make mother rest.
13. tell walt's father and your father to call.
14. sioux city, iowa
15. the netherlands, the rhineland, the ruhr valley
16. i live on the south side on merwin avenue.
17. the culture of the east is older than that of the west.
18. the south is the nation's winter playground.
19. turn north on 71 and go west at 306.
20. the senior class will graduate at severance hall.
21. among the books I enjoyed this year are *the kingdom and the power* by gay talese. this book describes the lives and ideas of the men who shaped the *new york times.*
22. when old man winter begins to play tricks in march, springing up with snow one day and bright sunshine the next, you know that spring is on the way.
23. the psalms reflect every possible emotion human beings can experience toward god. they do not mention jesus christ because they were written before his birth.

132   **Capitalization**

24. please tell dad that I will be late and I'll tell your mom that we'll be over for dinner, okay, buddy?
25. while I enjoy some of stravinsky's early works, I do not like "the firebird," nor do I care for debussy's tone poems.
26. I only want to remind you, ladies and gentlemen, to have your tickets to *the sheik* starring rudolph valentino ready.
27. at the museum we saw el greco's *toledo*, giotto's *virgin at the incarnation*, monet's *water lilies*, picasso's *man with sheep* and sculpture like rodin's *the thinker*, moore's *the family* and dali's *last supper*.
28. picasso is said to have gone through several phases in his painting—the blue period 1901-1904, the rose period 1905-1906, the négro period 1906-1908, and the cubist, classic and egyptian periods 1909-1918.
29. eugene o'neill wrote many plays, among them *anna christie*, *the great god brown*, *desire under the elms*, *the hairy ape*, a trilogy called *mourning becomes electra*, *emperor jones* and an autobiographical drama, *long day's journey into night*.
30. the secretary of state stepped out of a lincoln continental to board the vulcan for south america.
31. students of sino studies find they must study the chou, han, t'ang, sung, yuan and ming dynasties, the opium wars, the first and second sino-japanese war, the u.s. open door policy, the boxer rebellion, several civil wars, the great revolution and the soviet-chinese pact.
32. cole porter wrote songs which have entered permanently into america's heart: "what is this thing called love?" "just one of those things," and "begin the beguine."
33. Does captain kangaroo actually indulge in the mouth-watering tartness of sunkist oranges, the snap, crackle and pop of kellogg's rice krispies, the restored freshness of wonder bread and the smokey flavor of swift's bacon?
34. the sugar act, the currency act, the stamp act, the townshend acts and the tea act were the remote reasons why the colonists called the first continental congress.
35. step to the right, grandma, so that you are behind dad, and mom, you move over a little to the left of the twins.
36. the letter from uncle fred began: dear jennifer.

ONEOFTHEMOSTIMPORTANTSKILLSPEOPLEALLOVERTHEWORLD
WANTTOACQUIREISTHEABILITYTOCOMMUNICATETHEIRIDEAS
INWRITINGBUTEVENIFTHEYHAVEAGOODVOCABULARYAND
PERFECTSPELLINGTHEIRWRITINGWILLBEASHARDASTHISTOREAD
IFTHEYOMITCAPITALSANDTHOSETINYMARKSTHATMEANALOT
PUNCTUATION.

    Because words running together make little sense, the most important thing to master is grouping words to form sense-making units — sentences. To do that, follow these simple rules.
    Three end marks signal the end of sense-making units that can stand by themselves: periods, question marks and exclamation points.

Punctuation: End Marks

A period marks the end of a sentence — a group of words with a subject and verb that can stand alone and make sense.

Statement: The child picked up its toys.

Command: Put away your toys, Kim.

Indirect question: He asked if I was going.

Courtesy request: Will you pass the salt.

A question mark signals the end of a direct question.

Direct question: Are you coming?

Often question words introduce questions: *who, what, when, where, why, whom*. Other words that begin questions are the auxiliary verbs: *is, are, do, have, has, can, should*.

Who is that in the corner?

Have you heard about the accident?

An exclamation point shows surprise or strong emotion.

Jump!

Not on your life!

Let me out of here!

It may follow a word, a phrase or a sentence.

What end marks are needed for these sentences?

1. Will you please close the door
2. A man asked me where the station is
3. Did you tell him the news
4. He had no answer to the question: Are you ready to die
5. How wonderful that you got the job
6. The sun is shining and all is well in the world
7. Drop that gun or I'll shoot
8. Would you mind shutting that window; I'm cold
9. Were you worried about those questions
10. Do you think the main character is evil
11. Now wait a minute, young lady
12. Will the next witness please take the stand

13. May I have a reply by next week
14. Don't forget to remind me to stop at eleven
15. Leave the door open when you come in
16. Do you listen regularly to WYXY
17. The FBI wants you
18. The manuscript dates back to 10 BC
19. The Rev Francis Smith will address the group
20. My full name is Clark Clark, Jr

Arrange your own signals by writing original sentences:

1. asking someone to adjust a shade
2. informing a friend that his basement is full of water
3. telling the police about a burglar in your home
4. offering to carry a bag of groceries for an elderly person
5. complaining of a dropped dime

INTRA-SENTENCE PUNCTUATION

Correct punctuation of clauses within compound sentences is another way to separate meanings in groups of words. Independent clauses that can stand alone as sentences can be joined into a compound sentence in only three ways.

Join two independent clauses by a comma and a coordinating conjunction. | The golfers strolled on the green, **and** the caddies followed.

The coordinating conjunctions are *and, but, for, nor, or* and *yet*. A comma alone is not strong enough to hold two independent clauses together; however, a series of short clauses can be joined by commas.

no: We went to a picnic, the ants came too.

yes: It rained, the fire went out, the baby got lost, and we came home.

Join two independent clauses with a semicolon and one of the joining adverbs. | Washington was an excellent organizer; **moreover,** he was a warm person.

The joining adverbs are *nevertheless, however, therefore, consequently, thus, also, besides, furthermore, indeed, nonetheless, still, yet, at the same time, on the other hand, otherwise, for example, too.* Note that the joiner can come later in the second clause. If it interrupts the natural flow of the sentence, it is set off by commas.

Washington was an excellent organizer; he was, **at the same time,** a warm person.

Join two independent clauses that are closely related in meaning by a semicolon. | In his youth he was known for his honesty; in maturity he was still honest.

Review the three ways to join independent clauses. If these sentences are punctuated correctly, write C. If not, write the correct mark of punctuation and the word that should precede it.

1. Good eating does not consist of much eating, it consists of eating the right foods.
2. Even though all foods are different; after they are digested, they break down into the same nutrients.
3. These nutrients are; protein for growth and repair, carbohydrates for immediate energy, fat for reserve energy. And minerals and vitamins for regulating body processes.
4. Meat, fish, cheese and eggs are excellent sources of protein; cereal, bread and pastas provide carbohydrates; butter, egg yolk and fatty portions of meat give fats.
5. Fruits and vegetables are the main sources of vitamins and minerals, you should have some every day.
6. Oranges, grapefruit and tomatoes, for instance, are rich in vitamin C which strengthens blood vessels.
7. Yellow vegetables like pumpkin, squash and carrots contain vitamin A for resistance to colds and healthy eyesight, dark greens like parsley and spinach do the same.

Punctuation: Compound Sentences   137

8. The large vitamin B family; vitamin B_1, B_2, B_6 and B_{12} regulate the nervous system, they are found in abundance in cereals, enriched bread and lean meat.

9. Liver, raisins, prunes and dates are the best sources of iron; which is needed for healthy red blood.

10. Milk, of course, and cheese; as well as leafy green vegetables have large amounts of calcium and phosphorus for strong teeth and bones.

Write three complete sentences about the two photos using coordinating conjunctions. Write three using joining adverbs. Write three using only semicolons as joiners.

"Wee Paws"

In speaking, a slight drop in voice accompanied by a pause indicates the need for a comma in writing. Commas have two main purposes—to set off and to separate.

Commas are used to separate three or more elements of the same kind used in a series.

Words: He liked mushrooms, pepperoni, peppers and oregano on his pizza.

Phrases: We searched in the river, along the shoreline and in the forest.

Short Clauses: The men played cards on the porch, the women shot pool in the basement and the children romped in the yard.

A series can consist of words, phrases or clauses. The last item of the series is joined by *and* or *or* which may replace the comma.

Rewrite these sentences supplying needed commas.

1. Was the UFO red blue yellow or green?
2. The tall boy was always bumping his head on door jambs ducking to get into cars and crouching to allow others behind him to see.
3. For dinner Jim had two burgers Joe had three and Marty had four.
4. Doris wanted a committee chairman who was sensible responsible serious and likable.
5. A crowded noisy dirty airport gives visitors an unpleasant first impression of a city.
6. The couple made slow progress toward the park ambling leisurely down the avenue whispering occasionally to each other and laughing a good deal of the time.
7. Dragons in St. George's day were ugly challenging dangerous and conquerable.
8. The plane flew over New England the Eastern seaboard the Appalachian Mountains and part of the Gulf of Mexico.

9. A tall mysterious husky gentleman approached.
10. Gardening painting playing the trumpet and wrestling were among his interests.

Two or more equal adjectives before a noun should be separated by commas. | She bought an expensive, plush dining room set.

You can tell whether the adjectives are equal by substituting *and* for the commas. If the substitution does not make sense, do not use the comma.

Write any word after which a comma should fall.

The bright golden beauty of the wheat field blinded him. The wind sighed and whispered through the tall dry stalks. Soft pillowy clouds hung lazily in the deep blue sky while a combine tractor from a distance whirred growled and chewed. Slowly unconsciously easily Tom drifted into a world of peace stillness and utter beauty. Some time later as he came to he heard the snap of a twig beside him. "Dan where'd you come from?" he asked.

Write a sentence using adjectives before a noun.

Write original series to fill the blanks.

1. ____ are the kinds of dogs I know.
2. My favorite cars include ____.
3. In basketball (or football or volleyball) a player must master the skills of ____.
4. ____ were among the strengths of George Washington.
5. Barbara Walters' conversations reveal that she ____

Compose three sentences using adjectives, adverbs and verbs in a series. Compose two sentences using phrases and clauses.

Commas separate an appositive (identifier) from the word it explains.

Appositive: The child, the last of seven, was spoiled rotten.

If the appositive is closely connected, it is not separated.

My Aunt Mary isn't feeling well.

Steinbeck's novel *Grapes of Wrath* won the Pulitzer Prize.

Identify identifiers with commas.

1. Lageos a new two-foot solid metal ball covered with mirrors is a satellite that could be the most durable ever launched.
2. Lageos short for Laser Geodesic Satellite weighs 900 pounds.
3. It will be a target for earth-based laser signal reflections a tool for earthquake predictions.
4. The satellite only a dense sphere has no electronic or mechanical parts to get out of order.
5. Space agency officials predict it will last a long time from 50 to 100 years.

Commas separate introductory elements from the rest of the sentence.

Words: Yes, I think you should get red drapes.

Other introductory words include *well, no, of course, still, gosh, goodness.*

Transitional phrases: On the other hand, I'm not sure he's certified.

Other transitional phrases include: *In the first place, as mentioned before, secondly, finally* and others.

Participle phrases: Radiating compassion and sincere warmth, the President pinned the medal on the vet.

Introductory adverbial clause: Because he had been a whiz at logarithms, everyone thought he should be able to add.

For clarity: Still, as the leaf fell from the branch, I pondered my fate.

Introduce yourself to these by writing all words after which a comma should come.

1. Goodness the room is hot.
2. Yes I think I'll take these.
3. In the first place why were the children out at 9:30?
4. While driving Morris stopped for meals.
5. Well I for one don't agree.
6. Why what makes you think I'm upset?
7. Why can't the door be left open?
8. Secondly the supply affects the demand.
9. Moreover any sort of job discrimination is illegal.
10. In fact the people named were nowhere near the scene.

Commas show an omission in a second clause with the same structure.	In spring he played football; in winter, basketball.

The comma after *winter* takes the place of *he played*.

Use commas to set off elements that interrupt the natural flow of a sentence.	She is, **nevertheless**, your cousin. **Randy**, catch the baby. The cat, **smiling slyly**, stole the cheese.

1. Parenthetical elements

   Words: We will, **however**, pay your fare.

   Phrases: The club officers, **on the other hand**, did not agree.

   Clauses: His salary, **I believe**, is $20,000 a year.

Punctuation: Commas

2. Contrasting elements signaled by such words as *not* and *but not*

    Phyllis, **not June,** will emcee the program.

3. Items in direct address

    Ed, will you close the door.

    Will you, **Ed,** close the door.

    Will you close the door, **Ed.**

4. Participle phrases that are unnecessary

    Daphne, **gasping for breath,** crossed the finish line.

5. Clauses that are unnecessary

    George, **who prepared supper every day,** was an expert cook.

Who was an expert cook? George. The interrupting clause does not identify the subject. Necessary clauses are not set off by commas.

    The guy who prepared supper every day was an expert cook.

Which guy? The one who prepared supper. Here the clause identifies the subject.

When phrases or clauses are unnecessary, the subject is already identified fully before the addition. Usually clauses that modify proper nouns are unnecessary clauses. Those that identify common nouns are usually necessary. *That* introduces necessary clauses, and *which* usually introduces unnecessary clauses.

Decide whether these italicized clauses and phrases are necessary or unnecessary. Tell where commas should be used.

1. We included in our plans *of course* a ride on the trolley.
2. We were advised to take the one marked St. Charles *not St. Lawrence.*
3. As we waited *however* we noticed people gathering at a stop across the street to catch an approaching trolley.
4. We panicked and ran *as you can imagine* right through the traffic.

5. And reaching the other side *you guessed it* we made it for the St. Lawrence just as the St. Charles trolley came chugging to the stop we'd been standing at before we crossed.

Conventional Uses

1. Use commas to separate the second and each succeeding element of *address* in a sentence from the first.

           1
We toured London.

           1   2
We toured London, England.

           1   2   3
We toured Trafalgar Square, London, England.

2. Use commas to separate the second and each succeeding element of a *date* from the first.

           1
In 1948 he turned eighteen.

           1   2
On August 27, 1948, he turned eighteen.

3. Set off titles following a name by commas.

    Mrs. Ann Bishop, M.S.   Mr. R. Richaby, Jr.

4. Use a comma after the salutation of a friendly letter.

    Dear Angie,

5. Use a comma after the complimentary close of any letter.

    Sincerely yours,   Yours very truly,

Follow the rules to punctuate these sentences.

1. Letitia was born on September 7 1950 in Chattanooga Tennessee.

144 Punctuation: Commas

2. In November or December of that year her father bought their first home; twenty years later their second and last.
3. In 1975 she married a young man from Athens Greece.
4. The first cousins came from Tucson Arizona; the second from Birmingham Alabama.
5. Mark the address—Mr. henry Harland Sr. 2297 Winter Drive Apartment 3 Winterhaven Florida.

Write these sentences putting in any commas that are needed.

1. Good grief Maxine I left the matches at home.
2. How could you you you idiot?
3. Well I guess I was worried about that radiator hose.
4. All that charcoal all those steaks ears of corn potatoes and marshmallows and you forgot the matches. Bill sometimes I wonder about you.
5. Look I can drive down to the delicatessen. It'll only take a few minutes.
6. You mean that little store about fifty miles back?
7. It wasn't that far back Max.
8. Man if you think I'm going to sit here alone and wait for you, you're mistaken.
9. Well then come along.
10. Oh no Bill look the radiator is smoking!

Which phrases or clauses need commas? They are identified for you in the first five sentences. After that you're on your own.

1. The cab *that drove me to the airport* had one other passenger.
2. The driver *who wore a jaunty hat* told interesting stories all the way.
3. *Smiling jovially* he called out my fare as I prepared to leave.
4. I searched nervously for my wallet *which was deep in my handbag*.
5. He accepted my tip *grinning from ear to ear*.
6. "Sir would you help me get my luggage," I asked.
7. "Of course lady," he answered.
8. The luggage which held all my books for summer school gave even this burly man some trouble.

9. A redcap who was waiting at the curb to help took charge immediately.
10. Jan Smithers whom I had known since childhood was at the desk to say good-bye.
11. Lightning struck the high wires shutting off lights all over the town.
12. An electronics power company which specialized in restoring power systems was called in.
13. The company using computers to reroute energy applied its technical know-how.
14. Within minutes the systems suffering the breakdown were restored.
15. The city cloaked in darkness was once again a city of light.
16. Marty calling long distance spoke twenty minutes to me last night.
17. The bill amounting to $2.42 was to be paid by Marty.
18. A bill for $2.42 came to my house instead.
19. The phone representative apologizing for the error corrected my bill.
20. Marty paid the bill sent him the following month.

How's your comma sense? Remember, too many commas are as bad as too few.

1. Money invested is money, that you put to work to make more money.
2. Making investments is for people, who have stable income, a cash reserve for emergencies, regular savings, and some money to spare.
3. The wise investor seeking growth in capital-gains dollar income, and safety for his investment, may invest in income-producing assets in durable goods or in himself.
4. Securities ownership in a business or ownership of real estate, comes under income-producing investments.
5. Securities include bonds and stocks, which are usually issued, to obtain monies for production operation, or expansion.
6. Although some investors choose to put their money in commodities futures experts agree, that this is a high risk investment.
7. You must be aware, that you can if things go wrong lose considerable money.

MORE TO COME...

Colons and dashes have similar functions but almost opposite meanings in sentences. **Colons** point ahead: something is coming. **Dashes** point in the opposite direction—back to something that has already been said. Study the rules for these two marks of punctuation and try the exercises.

Use a colon before a list of three or more items especially after expressions such as as follows *and the* following, *but not directly after verbs.*	The fruit basket contained **the following:** pears, oranges, bananas, grapes, pineapples and three bottles of wine. The fruit basket contained pears, oranges, bananas....
Use a semicolon to separate items in a series that already include commas.	In the past eight years, we've lived in Boise, Idaho; Reno, Nevada; Toledo, Ohio; Newton, Massachusetts and Houston, Texas.

Write these sentences inserting needed punctuation.

1. Giving first aid to a patient not only includes knowing how to handle wounds, sprains, shock, fainting, bites, burns, poisoning and sunstroke, but it also includes the ability to apply artificial respiration.
2. The symptoms of shock include the following pale color, cold hands, weak breathing and faint pulse.
3. Fainting has the same symptoms with the exception of pulse which is rapid.
4. The treatment for fainting is to elevate the legs for drowning, to place patient on stomach and apply artificial respiration for acid burns, to use baking soda and then oil for alkali burns to use vinegar and then oil for severe bleeding to apply pressure to pressure points.
5. The signs of choking are turning blue, gasping and losing consciousness.

6. Choking can best be relieved by standing behind the victim, putting your arms around his midsection with one hand over the other and suddenly "hugging" him air forced up from his diaphragm will make the foreign object pop out.
7. Poisoning can be counteracted in these ways if severe rush the victim to the emergency room for stomach pumping if mild administer an emetic and soothing liquids such as eggs and milk.
8. Sunstroke requires rest, cold applications to the skin and no stimulants.
9. For heat exhaustion do the following make the patient rest and give stimulants but no cold applications.
10. The Red Cross is offering first aid classes to be held on Wednesday, March 19 Friday, March 21 Monday, March 24 Tuesday, March 25 Thursday, March 27 and Monday, March 31.

Conventional uses of colons

1. After the salutation of a business letter: Gentlemen:
2. Between hours and minutes written in figures: 3:25 a.m.
3. Between volume and number or volume and pages in a reference:
   Commonweal 27:36   *Commonweal* 27:35-48
4. Between chapter and verse in references to the Bible: Matt. 9:14-27

Write a business letter to a library. In it arrange a meeting at a particular time and request a particular issue of a magazine you need.

Use a dash to signal an abrupt break in thought or construction. | The price — I almost forgot to tell you! — is $400.

Too many dashes give the impression of childishness and emotionalism. Be conservative.

Use a dash in place of a comma for emphasis. | I dislike one food very much — ice cream.

Use a dash to mean for example, in other words, that is, before an explanation.

He is very neat—he polishes his shoes every day.

Where would you use dashes in these sentences?

1. The assets at the fall meeting excuse me my phone is buzzing.
2. Do you know Garrett Garrett what a name?
3. Bernie is my best friend at least five years ago he was.
4. Michelle Trelson you remember her just got her masters degree in archaeology.
5. I ran into a fellow I haven't seen for years.

Use parentheses to enclose interrupting information added to a sentence.

I am enclosing my check for fifteen hundred dollars ($1500).

If punctuation belongs to the parenthetical material, place it inside the parentheses; if not, place it outside.

We're preparing for the supervisor (as you already know).

She just won a new Buick (how I envy her!) and a yacht.

Independent parenthetical sentences are punctuated like other sentences.

The psalms are ancient prayer-songs. (They are incredibly beautiful, don't you agree?)

Where would parentheses be appropriate?

1. Because her stocking was filled with coal what else should she have expected? she was angry all day.
2. We saw that movie a year ago. Don't tell Rick He insists it's been longer.

3. The heavyweight champ he's now flabby and out of shape will meet his first contender in two years.
4. He paid I can't believe it seventy dollars for his hat.
5. She has fallen into the idiotic habit of tagging everything she says I wish I had the nerve to tell her with "you know."

Italics are right-slanting print. With the right pen, you can write in italics, too. But generally, in handwritten or typed script, they are shown by a single underline.

> **PLATIGNUM ITALIC SET**
>
> *Contains a fountain pen, five Italic nibs, and instruction manual, all for only $5.00... At art material & pen shops, college book stores...or send check to Pentalic Corp., 132 West 22 St., N.Y., N.Y. 10011 Add 50 cents for handling.*

Use italics for titles.

books: *Inside Africa*

newspapers: the *Chicago Tribune*

plays: *A Doll's House*

magazines: *Family Circle*

motion pictures: *Gone with the Wind*

long musical compositions: *Emperor Concerto*

works of art: *Mona Lisa*

long poems: *The Faerie Queene*

ships: *HMS Pinafore*

aircraft: *Boeing 747*

Punctuation: Italics

Use italics for words, letters and figures referred to as such. | How often did you use *namely*?
The *g* and *s* were lost in the printing.

Put foreign words in italics. | We wished him a *bon voyage*.

What should be italicized in these sentences?

1. During the eight-day voyage on Italia she read The Pirate by Robbins, Lady by Tryon and Here at the New Yorker by Gill.
2. The magazines in the dentists' office were a little dated: Life, Saturday Evening Post and Look.
3. His wide appreciation of music was obvious from his albums which included Appalachian Spring by Aaron Copland, Symphony No. 3 by Charles Ives, the Pastoral Symphony of Beethoven, Honky Tonk by Knuckles O'Toole, Anticipation by Carly Simon and Farewell Andromeda by John Denver.
4. Which paper do you read, the New York Times, The Christian Science Monitor or the Washington Post?
5. Voila! Here is the piece de résistance of dinner.

Write a brief description of this picture, giving both ships names.

Use quotation marks to show a change in language level. | In the garage person's lingo, I took my Cadillac in to get "juiced up."

Changes in level of language include technical terms in non-technical writing, colloquial words in formal writing, slang or other words used for special effect.

Use quotation marks to enclose the title of short works. | **articles:** "The Rise of James Reston on the *New York Times*"

songs: "My Old Kentucky Home"

chapters of a book: "Beachcombers"

poem: "Birches"

short plays: "Twelve Angry Men"

essays, short stories: "The Purloined Letter"

Where are quotation marks needed?

1. When frustrations mount and enemies multiply, when enterprises fall and friends betray, rant not, rave not; just hunker down and cool it for a space.
2. Victor Herbert wrote the old classic, Smoke Gets in Your Eyes.
3. Faulkner worked his short story The Bear into a novelette.
4. His article, The Three-Million-Year-Old Skeleton, caused a stir in scientific circles.

Hyphens

Hyphens are shorter than dashes. They are used to show how a word is divided. If you must break a word at the end of a line, use a hyphen at the end of the line.

I regret that I must interrupt my lecture now.

Generally, words are broken between syllables or between two consonants. Check your dictionary if you are uncertain about where to break a word. Never separate just one letter from the rest of the word. Other conventional uses of hyphens include these.

1. Hyphenate compound numbers 21-99.

    He started at twenty-five dollars a week.

2. Hyphenate a fraction used as an adjective or adverb.

    His tank was two-thirds full.

    but: Fill my tank to two thirds of its capacity.

3. Hyphenate a compound modifier preceding a noun.

    The new-born colt was wobbly on his legs.

    but: That colt is new born.

4. When two nouns form one word, connect them with a hyphen.

    The secretary-treasurer was absent.

5. Use a hyphen after *re-* to distinguish two words that might be confused.

    Will you re-sort these envelopes?

Where are hyphens needed?

1. In playing Careers, she began with twenty seven thousand dollars and ended in jail.
2. The poet journalist was torn between his desire to resort all his poems for publication and to recreate his society along truly democratic lines.
3. His temperament was four fifths gentle but friends learned to beware the remaining one fifth.
4. The director's half baked ideas resulted in confusion, frustration and failure.
5. The near and sub zero temperatures caused widespread crop failure.

Review the punctuation marks by writing this paragraph.

Lagolago Mulitaupele she is the Samoan exchange student I told you about waited impatiently for her family to arrive. The Australian liner Melbourne was docking as we watched in the warm lakefront smog. Suddenly Lag we call her that for short broke into a wide smile and waved. I trembled almost as if Mozart's Jupiter Symphony were racing through my brain. There they are she shouted. I looked. A short stocky bronzed figure appeared. He was wearing at first I couldn't believe my eyes only a lava-lava and sandals of course. In his right hand he held a staff which he used almost like a bishop's crook but except for his proud upright bearing he was a far cry from a bishop. Here was Anomoto Mulitaupele we learned later he was called Chief Pele the chief and mayor of a large city in Samoa in all his native splendor coming to meet his long unseen daughter. I watched spellbound as he approached. Neither he nor she seemed to notice the hundreds of eyes upon them. Then he was there five feet in front of her and bending from the waist his hand still high on his staff. He bowed royally. And she this twenty year old Americanized Samoan curtsied primly in formal greeting of her august father.

APOSTROPHE

Add **'s** *to form the possessive of singular nouns.*

| my brother**'s** coat |
| the child**'s** toy |
| Thomas**'s** gloves |
| Dickens**'s** stories |

To form the possessive of plural nouns ending in **s** add only the apostrophe.

    her two brothers**'** cars   the two Charleses**'** watches

Add **'s** to form the possessive of plural nouns that do not end in **s.**

    the men**'s** shop   the three mice**'s** squeals   people**'s** sorrow

154   Punctuation: Apostrophes

Use an apostrophe to show the omission of letters and figures.	can't	isn't
	won't	Spirit of '76

Keep the original uncontracted words the same except for **won't** and **doesn't**.

Write the singular possessive, the plural and the plural possessive for each of these, using the item given as the thing possessed.

1. fence — length
2. book — theme
3. week — pay
4. goose — honk
5. nail — head
6. Gail — last name
7. Thomas — vacation
8. cup — handle
9. fox — snout
10. church — belfry
11. woman — purse
12. cousin — money
13. sheep — wool
14. Jones — car
15. butterfly — wings
16. star — distance
17. dictionary — cover
18. brush — bristle
19. people — houses
20. bench — hardness

Rewrite each phrase as a possessive.

1. the purse of the girl
2. the jokes of a friend
3. the work of an hour
4. the hideout of a panther
5. the coat of Mike
6. the poetry of Keats
7. the car of Mrs. Evans
8. the cat of the Reillys

Indefinite pronouns—those pronouns that do not refer to a specific antecedent—do require an apostrophe to show possession. Never use an apostrophe with a possessive pronoun.

It was **everyone's** responsibility.

It was his responsibility.

Whose hat is on the table?

Change the words in the parentheses into possessive form.

1. They liked the (outfits of each other).
2. At the seance we all held (the hands of one another).
3. I think I just sat on (the hat of someone).
4. The (bottle of this twin) is cold. Check if (the bottle belonging to the other one) is too.
5. Is it (the responsibility of no one)?
6. Indeed, it is (the duty of everyone).
7. This coat must be (that of someone else).
8. This is the (table of that waitress).
9. It was the (reaction of the press).
10. These are (the poems of Stevens).

Correct any errors in the following sentences.

1. Who's pie is this?
2. That pie is her's.
3. I thought it was yours.
4. This one is our's.
5. It's crust is flaky and brown.
6. So is theirs.
7. These are someone elses' rubbers.
8. Those are the boss' orders.
9. That is nobody's business.
10. We shared one anothers' sorrow.

Rewrite the possessive if it is incorrectly formed.

Can I use someone's suntan lotion? Mine's in my beach bag down in the lockers. Its funny but I never have it when I want it. Isnt Beths bathing suit an unusual color? Who's blanket is this? Can I use it? Oh for goodness's sake, I think I just sat on somebodies' sun glasses. Did you say they are Charle's? He's going to kill me. If their prescription, it'll take three week's pay to get together enough money. You say their light adjustable? Just my luck. Too bad I din't choose Karen's and Thomas's blanket to sit on. Then things wouldn't of turned out this way.

If each member in the group gives his or her hat to the person on the left and the last person in the top row gives it to the first on the lower right, write a paragraph telling who is wearing whose hat.

PUNCTUATING DIALOGUE

Follow these seven rules when you are writing dialogue or any direct quotations.

1. Use quotation marks to enclose a direct quotation.

   "We will win," said the coach.

2. When a dialogue tag interrupts a direct quotation, close quotes before the tag and open them again after it.

   "We will win," said the coach, "and go to State."

3. A direct quotation is set off from the rest of the sentence by commas or by a question mark or exclamation point.

   Kelly whined, "Where, oh where has my little dog gone?"

   "Where, oh where, has my little dog gone?" Kelly whined.

4. Commas and periods are always placed inside closing quotation marks.

   Jessie cried, "I snagged my stocking."

5. Colons and semicolons are always placed outside closing quotation marks.

   After winning, Chris smiled and bragged, "It was a snap"; but at his locker he admitted he'd had his moments of doubt.

6. Question marks and exclamation points are placed inside the closing quotation marks if the quotation is a question or exclamation. Otherwise they are placed outside.

   Did you quote the Little Prince when you said each person is "unique in all the world"?

   "Are you going, Sam?" I asked.

7. Begin a new paragraph for the words of each new speaker.

   "Millie," called Steve, as he paced back and forth through the foyer and living room.

   "What do you want?" returned Millie.

Set each paragraph up as a dialogue, indenting and putting in quotation marks. Insert any missing punctuation.

1

"Help! Can someone please help?" I called from the manhole I'd fallen into. A dog peered over the edge, perked his ears, barked a single and emphatic "Arf!" and disappeared. "Help!" I shouted again as I tried to reach the edge of the hole with my fingertips. "I think I heard someone yell help," I heard a lady say, but then her voice and footstep died away. "Hello up there," I screamed even louder. "I'm down in the manhole." An old gentleman bent over but his figure must have thrown a shadow over me for he straightened and left before I could speak. "Hello," I repeated. "Hello. Helloooo."
"Did someone say hello," a young girl asked leaning over the edge of the manhole.
"Yes," I said, eagerly. "It's me."
"Goodness. How did you get down there?" she asked.
"I fell in," I said humiliated. "Could you help me out?"
"Well, what can I do?"
"Just give me a hand," I said. She reached in. I caught her hand and pulled hard. I pulled so hard she lost her balance and there we were.
"Help!" we shouted.

2

"Ellery," said Inspector Queen. "There is only one clue. The victim pulled out the clock and TV cord just before she died."
"Dad, you know I have a deadline to make. I just can't take the case."
"Well, all right, I just thought . . . . Did you say both cords? Now she was an intelligent girl. She was trying to tell us something. All you have to do is find out what she was trying to say. I knew you'd come up with something, Ellery."
"Dad I'm *not* working on this case. You'll have to figure it out for yourself. Did you say the clock stopped at 10:25?"
"Yes, that's what we found."
"Did you check what was on at 10:25 the night of the murder, Dad? It'll probably contain the answer."
"Right. Why didn't I think of that?" Inspector Queen asked himself aloud. "Ellery why is it you always come up with the right answer, when it seems there are no clues at all?"
"Because I use my common sense, I am observant and I notice details," Ellery bragged as he headed for the door. "But now I have to go or my publisher will throw a fit."
"Ellery, you forgot your glasses," said Inspector Queen.

3

It was December 7 1941 and the worshippers were quietly preparing for the service. The minister appeared at the pulpit. My people I have a serious message for you this morning he began. The nation is at war. This morning the President has announced that the Army Navy Air Corps and Marines are to be prepared to receive orders at any moment. Yes our worst expectations have been realized We are no longer a peaceful friendly nation We are a nation at war. Are we ready to suffer Are we willing to pay the price Let us dear friends offer our petitions that our combat may be brief and our cause victorious Shall we begin today's service with the hymn on page 39.

Write each sentence on your paper, inserting punctuation.

1. I said Marie wearily am going to bed
2. I asked myself the question when are you going to learn
3. I think Gloria is a bit neurotic she washes her hands three times an hour but otherwise she's efficient
4. I like to rise as the saying goes with the chickens
5. John remarked Fridays are the best days
6. I said to him Would you please close the door
7. She read a two volume encyclopedia and a thirty page magazine for her eight page paper
8. I enjoy knitting and crocheting
9. John likes Mary Jane his brother prefers Dolores
10. How splendid that you won the scholarship
11. My dear Susan
12. Yours very truly
13. Would you type this letter by tonight
14. I bowled 225 however that was a miracle
15. The company has branches in Pueblo Colorado Phoenix Arizona and Billings Montana
16. Ford introduced something new in protection namely the whiplash seat
17. Georgia walked 24 miles and quit her sister walked 25.
18. All the stealing in the school boiled down to one person a freshman boy

19. Gentlemen
20. Ps 32 1-3
21. She has a teaching certificate in three areas biology home ec and English
22. A soiled towel a torn shoe string and a bloody hanky that was all we had to go on
23. One thing I love with a passion shoofly pie
24. And now may I introduce heavens there's been an explosion
25. William Shakespeare 1564-1616 is the world's greatest poet
26. Please send twenty five 25 shirts
27. We drank the milk which was slightly sour but refused the wine
28. Gail not Karen is coming
29. Marty didn't realize or so she said
30. Before he called anybody his amigo he wanted a pledge of loyalty
31. Mark liked kielbasi Polish sausage his sister preferred wieners
32. After a long walk Hansel and Gretel came to the house in the woods
33. It is an old saying that a penny saved is a penny earned
34. He is a statesman philosopher
35. They took a door to door survey
36. North American savages are extinct or are they
37. She is twenty one today
38. He gave away one half of his earnings
39. The wedding preparation was a six month affair
40. Winnie have you read Archy and Mehitabel by Don Marquis

The Latest Thing

Although "We'll Show You When We Come to Vote" would seem to be a suffragist's song, it had a different purpose. Notice that it was written by a man. What attitude do you think he was trying to show? Would you consider this satire?

We'll Show You When We Come To Vote

Song and Chorus by

Frank Howard

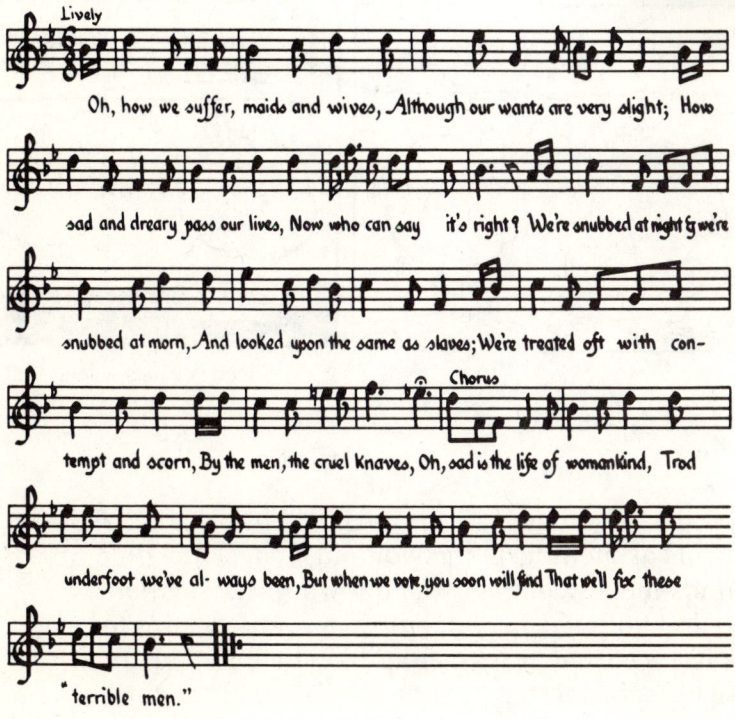

Oh, how we suffer, maids and wives, Although our wants are very slight; How sad and dreary pass our lives, Now who can say it's right? We're snubbed at night & we're snubbed at morn, And looked upon the same as slaves; We're treated oft with contempt and scorn, By the men, the cruel knaves, Oh, sad is the life of womankind, Trod underfoot we've al- ways been, But when we vote, you soon will find That we'll fix these "terrible men."

2. There's Mister Brady's pretty wife,
Although she lives in queenly style,
I know she leads a wretched life,
She seems sad all the while;
It's true she rides in her carriage fine,
And buys six dresses ev'ry week,
It's true she "gads about" all the time,
But of trifles we'll not speak, For
CHORUS

3. Of course we know each word is false,
That's said of Mistress William Brown,
That she so dearly loves to walk
And flirt about the town;
They say she leaves Mister B. alone,
And out to "suffrage circles" goes,
While he the little ones rocks at home,
Which I'm sure quite plainly shows, That
CHORUS

4. And when you hear my own sad case,
I know your hearts will bleed for me;
You can tell by my thin, careworn face,
How wretched I must be;
My husband gives me but once a week,
A hundred dollar bill to spend;
Of such cruelty I'll no farther speak,
But wont stand it long, depend, Oh,
CHORUS

If You Don't Know How to Spell It...

© 1975 United Feature Syndicate, Inc.

    Life would be easier if you could just "fake it," but that's no answer to the problems of spelling. Often, you must check the dictionary. Nobody minds looking up really far out words like *ukulele* or *Richelieu* which don't often come up, but who wants to have to look up words like *its*, *occurred* or *occasionally*, which pop up all the time. It's easier to learn the patterns of English. This chapter offers ways to improve your spelling habits. See how you do on a simple test.

1. The old man suffered from (lonliness, loneliness).
2. The office was (transfered, transferred) to New York.
3. (Whose, Who's) afraid of the big bad wolf?
4. Did you (receive, recieve) my letter?
5. I (already, all ready) (separated, seperated) the books.

If you found yourself hesitating over any of the answers, continue reading.

Begin by pronouncing words distinctly, breaking them into individual syllables. Watch prefixes and suffixes. You can even exaggerate to bring out difficult parts, especially silent letters or letters that are slurred in conversation.

Say

per form, not pre form.

sep a rate, not sep er ate.

re **cog** nize, not rec on ize.

dis as **trous**, not dis as ter ous.

at**h** let ic, not ath a let ic.

light **n**ing, not light en ing.

li **a** ble, not lible

drowned, not drown ded

Study these often mispronounced words with the help of the questions on page 164.

A	B	C
drow ned	pic ture (photo)	un ne cess ary
does n't	govern ment	boun dar y
strat e gy	veg e table	dis sat is fy
jewel ry	sher bet	pe cu li ar
math e matics	can di date	ce ler y
pro bab ly	soph o more	sim i lar
mar i tal (marriage)	chil dren	min i a ture
mar ti al (military)	mod ern	mis spell
mar ri age	nor thern	un nat ur al

1. Which words end in *ern*? *ren*?
2. Which words have in them the following words: *pic, spell, mat, jewel, drown, soph, bet, table, govern, bound*? What other shorter words do you find?
3. What is the difference between *peculiar* and *similar*?
4. Which letter would easily be forgotten in the following:

   boundary   misspell   vegetable   mathematics

   dissatisfy unnatural   candidate   marriage

   peculiar   government   sophomore   probably

Test your skill by identifying the correct spelling.

1. quantity, quanity
2. probably, probly
3. stragedy, strategy
4. marage, marriage
5. doesn't, dosen't
6. jewlry, jewlery, jewelry
7. marital, marial (wed)
8. mathmatics, mathematics
9. drowned, drownded
10. martial, marital (military)
11. celery, celry
12. unatural, unnatural
13. boundry, boundary
14. similiar, similar
15. peculiar, pecuilar

1. vegetable, vegtable
2. candidate, canidate
3. sophmore, sophomore
4. modern, modren
5. childern, children
6. sherbet, sherbert
7. suger, sugar
8. northren, northern
9. pitcher, picture (photo)
10. government, goverment
11. dissappoint, disappoint
12. disatisfy, dissatisfy
13. unnecessary, unecessary
14. minature, miniature
15. mispell, misspell

Silent Sounds

Training yourself to see letters that remain silent will help you spell a number of words. There are only a few beginning letters that are silent partners. Here are three that you will often meet: **ps, ph, pn.**

Which silent p combination should begin each of these words?

__ ychiatrist, __ ychology, __ ysician, __ ychiatric, __ ychological, __ osphates, __ ychic, __ ychedelic, __ osphorus, __ ychoanalysis, __ alm, __ ysical, __ eumonia, __ eumatic

What words do you know that begin with *wr, gh, ch, rh, kn*?

Sometimes the silent letters occur within a word. Which letters are silent in these?

im _ ediat _ ly, We _ nesday, fo _ rth, fo _ r, b _ y, g _ ardian, tho _ _ _ t, strai _ _ t, ha _ f, g _ ess, begin _ ing, tho _ _ _ , e _ rly, _ our, inste _ d, di _ _ theria, g _ ard, of _ en, cor _ _ , r _ ythm, debri _ , autum _ , hym _ , mor _ gage, s _ ord, ca _ f, de _ t, de _ tor, i _ le, i _ land, g _ est, ans _ er, rece _ _ t, nu _ sance, to _ ard, solem _ , colum _ , condem _ .

Ruler Derby

English spelling is probably the most difficult in the world. It has many rules and many exceptions. That's why learning a few basic rules will give you instant mastery over hundreds of words that you may hesitate over now. Don't forget to memorize the exceptions.

A single-syllable word ending in a consonant preceded by one vowel doubles the final consonant before adding a suffix beginning with a vowel.	trip + ed = tripped	slip + ery = slippery
	slim + est = slimmest	skip + ing = skipping
	gun + er = gunner	red + ish = reddish

Not two vowels: loan + ed = loaned
Not two consonants: limp + ing = limping
Not two syllables: alter + ed = altered

Spelling: Adding Suffixes

Two-syllable words accented on the second syllable and ending in a single consonant preceded by a single vowel double the final consonant to add a suffix beginning with a vowel.

excel + ed = excelled

excel + ing = excelling

but   profit + ed = profited (accent on first syllable)

but   benefit + ed = benefited (three syllables)

Try these.

1. Add *er*: win, trip, trim, rob, sad, sin, bet, slim, stop, grim
2. Add *ed*: pin, tip, slap, whip, fan, drop, strip, slim, rob, plan
3. Add *ing*: rib, drop, beg, sin, fan, clip, blur, war, bet, dot
4. Add *est*: slim, trim, grim, fat, hot

Write sentences to show you know the difference between the pairs.

Try writing the uninflected form of each word.

planned, planed	hoping, hopping
cuter, cutter	stripped, striped
starring, staring	gaping, gapping
mopping, moping	robbed, robed
caped, capped	taped, tapped

What sums do you get?

debit + ed	commit + ed
impel + ing	confer + ed
commit + ment	confer + ence
equip + ing	differ + ence
differ + ed	propel + ing
transmit + er	equip + ed
commit + ee	permit + ed
debit + ing	cream + ery

Write these paragraphs adding suffixes.

    1. Because we (plan) to hold a party, we (mop) the basement and (rob) the other rooms of tables and chairs before they (stop) us. We had the place (whip) into shape in no time.

    2. We (differ) in our opinions, but we were both (commit) to (begin) a project to benefit the poor. We knew it wasn't (permit) to use the (commit) members for any other than the (allot) purposes and so we (confer) with a lawyer before (plot) any action, however simple.

    Write a paragraph using five words governed by rule 2.

*When a word ends in **y** preceded by a consonant, change the **y** to **i** before adding any suffix that does not begin with **i**.*	fly + es = flies dry + er = drier fly + ing = flying but enjoy + ed = enjoyed (*y* not preceded by consonant) Exceptions: daily, gaily, slain, paid, said (*y* preceded by vowel)
*Single-syllable words ending in **y** preceded by a consonant retain the **y** before the suffixes -ly and -ness.*	slyness shyly

Write each new word.

hurry + ed	steady + ed	weary + est	busy + ness
sad + ly	gay + ly	hardy + est	cry + er
slay + ing	hasty + ness	lucky + er	pay + able
hazy + ly	defy + ed	spray + ed	busy + ly
rely + ing	cry + ing	spry + ness	shy + ness
shy + ly	lovely + ness	imply + ed	sky + ward
tasty + er	merry + est	glory + ous	baby + hood

Spelling: Adding Suffixes

Write this paragraph adding suffixes.

In those days, we (sad) (shy) away from directly (defy) authority, but we (rely) on influential friends to make the necessary changes. This (imply) having to be patient and (un-hurry) in our expectations, so we (busy) ourselves with other things while we waited.

> When a word ends in a silent **e**, preceded by a consonant, drop the **e** before adding a suffix beginning with a vowel.

pine + ing = pining   dine + er = diner

Keep the **e** before a suffix beginning with a consonant:

excite + ment = excitement   love + ly = lovely

Exceptions: awful, argument, acknowledgment, judgment, wholly, duly, truly, ninth.

Write the new word.

deceive + er   fame + ous
fuse + ing   love + able
grieve + ous   like + ing
value + able   lose + ing
insure + ing   pursue + er
move + able   manage + ment
excite + ing   insure + ance
grieve + ous   wry + ly
face + less   due + ly
grace + ful   awe + ful
require + ment   whole + ly
amuse + ment   judge + ment

Spelling: Adding Suffixes

scarce + ly
use + less
nine + ty
lone + ly

acknowledge + ment
nine + th
toe + ing
dye + ing

Add the correct suffixes to the words in parentheses.

The (dine) complained to the owner of the (dine) room that because his bowl was cracked he was (lose) his soup. A (continue) stream of the (value) liquid seeped through the crack. He protested that the soup was (true) good in his (judge) and he (whole) regretted having to miss any of the (love) taste. It was all (use). They threw him out!

How should each new word be spelled?

hope + ful
improve + ment
choose + ing
dine + ing
dine + er
write + ing
write + er
admire + able
value + ing
insure + ance

pine + ing
admire + ing
argue + ing
argue + ment
love + ly
love + able
due + ly
lonely + ness
sincere + ly
grate + ful

When a word ends in **ce** *or* **ge,** *keep the* **e** *before adding the suffixes* -able *and* -ous.

notice + able = noticeable

courage + ous = courageous

Only one word ends in **sede**: supersede. Three words end in **ceed**: *succeed, proceed, exceed.* All the rest end in **cede**: *accede, concede, secede, antecede, intercede, precede, recede.*

Spelling: Adding Suffixes

To retain the hard sound of words ending in **c**, add **k** before adding a suffix beginning with **e, i** or **y**.

| picnic + ing = picnicking |
| picnic + ed = picnicked |
| panic + y = panicky |

Write each new word.

change + able
super (cede, ceed, sede)
panic + y
manage + able
picnic + ing
ex (ceed, cede, sede)
re (ceed, cede, sede)
mimic + er
unchange + able
ac (cede, ceed, sede)
outrage + ous
se (ceed, cede, sede)
notice + able
traffic + ed

suc (cede, ceed, sede)
pre (cede, ceed, sede)
pro (cede, ceed, sede)
indulge + ence
grace + ious
re (ceed, cede, sede)
inter (ceed, cede, sede)
advantage + ous
frolic + ing
unmanage + able
courage + ous
critic + al
strange + er
arrange + ment

Keep the full word when adding prefixes and the suffixes -ness and -ly.

| dis + appoint = di**s**appoint |
| dis + satisfy = di**ss**atisfy |
| over + ripe = ove**rr**ipe |
| mis + spell = mi**ss**pell |
| accidental + ly = accidenta**ll**y |
| green + ness = gree**nn**ess |

Spelling: Adding Prefixes

Spell each new word correctly.

mis + spell	lean + ness
un + able	casual + ly
un + necessary	cool + ly
sub + marine	extensive + ly
il + legal	grim + ness
over + abundance	mean + ness
over + reaching	drunken + ness
un + noticeable	practical + ly
im + mature	foul + ly
re + collect	keen + ness

Add prefixes or suffixes to make sense of the paragraph.

(Grim), (mean), and (drunken) are three faults that make for (unneighborly). They are qualities of (mature). (Quiet), (open) and (keen), on the other hand, will never (appoint) your friends.

Write a paragraph using at least five of these words adding suffixes or prefixes.

usual + ly	open + ness
inter + cellular	mis + step
quiet + ness	un + neighborly
occasional + ly	il + legal
dis + satisfy	inter + relational
inter + racial	dis + appear
final + ly	im + mortal
in + active	over + ripe
dis + appoint	musical + ly
over + ride	green + ness

Spelling: I-E Rule

*Use **i** before **e** except after the letter **c** or before the combination **gh**.*

ach**ie**ve   c**ei**ling
bel**ie**ve   w**ei**gh

Exceptions: either, financier, neither, leisure, seize, weird

Write each word inserting the correct *i-e* combination.

bel _ _ f	w _ _ ght	n _ _ ther
sh _ _ ld	c _ _ ling	misch _ _ f
shr _ _ k	y _ _ ld	w _ _ rd
n _ _ ce	f _ _ ld	l _ _ sure
br _ _ f	v _ _ l	v _ _ w
ach _ _ ve	th _ _ r	financ _ _ r
fr _ _ ght	n _ _ ghbor	s _ _ ve
rec _ _ ve	s _ _ ge	_ _ ther
dec _ _ t	perc _ _ ve	s _ _ ze
conc _ _ ving	sl _ _ gh	fr _ _ nd

N _ _ ther his n _ _ ghbors nor a financ _ _ r could sh _ _ ld him from financial ruin. By a w _ _ rd twist of fate and dec _ _ tful partners his accounts had come to misch _ _ f. Soon he knew he would be rec _ _ ving welfare.

Write a paragraph using three words from the *i-e* group.

Overall review

recur + ed	write + ing
courage + ous	dye + ing
rec _ _ ve	s _ _ ze
dis + satisfy	comply + ing
mimic + ed	notice + able

Spelling: Foreign Words 173

fly + er

pin + ed

sale + able

prefer + ence

shy + ly

bel _ _ ve

green + ness

dine + er

transfer + ed

try + es

pro + (ceed, cede, sede)

w _ _ rd

gay + ly

argue + ment

refer + ed

study + ing

il + legal

whole + ly

suc + (cede, ceed, sede)

occur + ence

reply + ed

lone + liness

frolic + ed

love + able

mis + spell

grip + ing

gripe + ing

dis + appear

pre + (cede, ceed, sede)

s _ _ ve

judge + ment

due + ly

nine + th

duty + ful

will + full

true + ly

Notes from Abroad

Most foreign words that have come into the language now form their plurals by adding **s** or **es**.

Singular	Plural	Foreign Plural
appendix	appendixes	appendices
cactus	cactuses	cacti
antenna	antennas	antennae

But a few words keep their foreign plurals.

Singular	Plural
alumna (female)	alumnae
alumnus (male)	alumni
stimulus	stimuli
analysis	analyses
basis	bases
crisis	crises
emphasis	emphases
hypothesis	hypotheses
parenthesis	parentheses
thesis	theses
bacterium	bacteria
criterion	criteria
medium	media
phenomenon	phenomena

Make these foreign words plural.

1. They cultured the (bacterium) in petri dishes.
2. A number of inexplicable (phenomenon) scared the babysitter.
3. Did any of her (hypothesis) ever evolve into solid information?
4. The (analysis) of several experts working independently ended in the same conclusions.
5. He did not respond to any of the (stimulus).
6. The (medium) are influential in shaping public opinion.
7. The (alumnus) held a reunion.
8. What were the (basis) of your many suspicions?
9. His life held many tragic (crisis).
10. The judges had ten (criterion).
11. He wrote three (thesis) before one was accepted toward his degree.

The Latest Thing

"Come Home, Father!" is a kind of morality tale. What is the moral? What cause do you think the song was trying to promote?

Come Home, Father!
Words and Music by Henry C. Work

1. Father, dear father, come home with me now!
    The clock in the steeple strikes one;
You said you were coming right home from the shop,
    As soon as your day's work was done.
Our fire has gone out—our house is all dark—
    And mother's been watching since tea,
With poor brother Benny, so sick in her arms,
    And no one to help her but me.
Come home! come home! come home! Please, father,
    dear father, come home.

CHORUS:

Hear the sweet voice of the child. . . .
    Which the nightwinds repeat as they roam! . . .
Oh who could resist this most plaintive of prayers?
    "Please, father, dear father, come home!"

2. Father, dear father, come home with me now!
    The clock in the steeple strikes two;
The night has grown colder, and Benny is worse—
    But he has been calling for you.
Indeed he is worse—Ma says he will die,
    Perhaps before morning shall dawn;
And this is the message she sent me to bring—
    "Come quickly, or he will be gone."
Come home! come home! come home! Please, father,
    dear father, come home.

CHORUS:

3. Father, dear father, come home with me now!
    The clock in the steeple strikes three;
The home is so lonely—the hours are so long
    For poor weeping mother and me.
Yes, we are alone—poor Benny is dead,
    And gone with the angels of light;
And these were the very last words that he said—
    "I want to kiss Papa good night."
Come home! come home! come home! Please, father,
    dear father, come home.

CHORUS.

Spelling

There are words that you just have to study. This is a list of some of the most frequently misspelled words. Mastering them will be of lifelong benefit to you.

1	2	3	4	5
abundance	apparatus	comparative	discipline	foreign
accidentally	appropriate	conscientious	efficient	fulfill
accommodate	awkward	conscious	eliminate	gauge
achieve	bookkeeping	convenient	emphasize	hindrance
acknowledge	brilliant	criticism	endeavor	hurriedly
acquaintance	carburetor	curiosity	environment	immense
administration	changeable	desirable	especially	incidentally
advisable	character	despair	exhausted	indispensable
analyze	commercial	disappoint	expense	ingenious
anonymous	commission	disastrous	financial	interfere

6	7	8	9	10
irresistible	noticeable	perspiration	religious	sufficient
legitimate	nuisance	possess	repetition	superintendent
liable	obedience	prejudice	responsible	technical
maintenance	occasional	privilege	ridiculous	temperament
miniature	occurrence	procedure	scarcely	tendency
minimum	organization	professor	sensible	theory
miscellaneous	pamphlet	psychology	sergeant	tragedy
mischievous	peculiar	pursue	siege	typical
mortgage	perseverance	receipt	significant	villain
neighbor	persistent	recognize	success	weird

Index to Usage and Style

Language changes are reflected first in speech habits and then only slowly, and sometimes never, in writing. This index will help you decide when a word or expression is acceptable for your written work.

a, an *A* precedes words beginning with a consonant *sound: a bicycle, a utensil. An* is used before words with a vowel sound: *an apple, an ambition, an hour.*

accept, except *Accept* means "to receive." *Except* means "to leave out." *Because I accepted you in my class, I can't except from doing the work. Everyone except Ralph has left.*

adapt, adopt *Adapt* means "to change to fit," "to adjust." *Adopt* means "to take as one's own." *Will the adopted refugees adapt to the new culture?*

addition, edition An *addition* is something added; an *edition* is a form of book.

advice, advise *Advice* rhymes with **dice**; it is a noun. *The guidance counselor gave me some sound advice. Advise* rhymes with *guys. It is a verb. Will you advise me?*

affect, effect A verb, *affect* means "to influence," or "to put on a pretense of." *The lesson affected her efficiency.* A noun, *effect,* means "the result." *What effect will the surgery have on her eyes?*

ahold of Nonstandard for "hold of."

ain't Nonstandard contraction for *am not, is not, are not, have not, has not.* Used by educated people in fun, it "ain't" suitable for formal use.

allusion, illusion An *allusion* is an indirect reference: *Your allusion to Shakespeare is apt.* An *illusion* is a false idea: *She is under the illusion that she can win.*

all that (bad, great) Colloquial expression not suitable for formal writing.

all the farther, all the faster These phrases should not be used for *as far as* or *as fast as.*

almost, most See *most.*

a lot *Lot* is a noun meaning "a considerable quantity." *A* is the determiner that often precedes it. Think "a little, a lot, a whole lot." You will then never write *alot* as one word. *A lot* is informal and usually avoided in formal writing.

Make choices that are suitable for formal writing.

1. That was (all the farther, as far as) the car would go.
2. The rock concert couldn't have been (all that wild, as wild as you say).
3. We are planning to (adopt, adapt) the play for film.

4. He was (a, an) M.C. you'd never forget.
5. We planted (a lot, alot) of corn this year.
6. I couldn't get (ahold, hold) of the president.
7. What is the (affect, effect) of that drug?
8. If you want my (advice, advise), stay away from ragweed.
9. I can't (accept, except) your excuse.
10. How did it (affect, effect) you when you found you could (adapt, adopt) a refugee orphan?
11. Jeffrey has no (allusions, illusions) about his ability.
12. They are bringing out a new (edition, addition) of the dictionary.

already, all ready *Already* is an adverb meaning "now, prior to a given time." *Are you here already? All ready* means "entirely prepared." *The children were all ready to leave.*
alright, all right *Alright* is nonstandard. Think *all wrong, all right.*
altogether, all together *Altogether* is an adverb and means "entirely." *Mort looks altogether devastating in that hat. All together* means "everyone assembled." *The three choirs sang all together.*
among, between See *between.*
amount, number Countable items take *number: a large number of cartons. Amount* is for units: *the amount of sugar.*
ampersand, & The name of the sign *& (and).* Avoid this short cut and all other abbreviations except titles in all writing except private notes or technical lists. Always write out *and.*
analyzation Always incorrect for *analysis.*
an, and *An* is a determiner: *an evergreen, an MC. And* is a conjunction joining equal things: *toast and coffee.*
and, etc. A repetitious phrase. *Et cetera* means "and the like." Therefore, *and* is redundant. *And so forth* is more common.
as Avoid *as* to mean "because." *As I was working, she left.* Does *as* mean "while" or "because"? Do not use *as* for *that. I can't say as I enjoyed the music.*

1. It's (alright, all right), dear. Your mother will return.
2. We're (altogether, all together) again, thank heaven.

3. We bought items for the garden: a spray, a hoe, a rake, a spade, (and, etc.; etc.)
4. Punch (an, and) Judy were once popular puppets.
5. We waited until dusk, (&, and) then left.
6. He's (already, all ready) fifteen minutes late.
7. I can't say (as, that) I'm displeased.
8. Your (analyzation, analysis) of the characters is excellent.
9. Your donation of any (amount, number) of candy bars will be appreciated.
10. (As, Because) Mother was busy, I went into the garage.

anyway, anyways *Anyway* is the correct form. *Anyways* is colloquial.

anywheres, somewheres Always colloquial for *anywhere* and *somewhere*.

awake, wake *Awake* usually means "to become awake": *when I awake*. *Wake* usually means "to get someone up." *Will you wake her?*

awful, awfully *Awful* is colloquial for "very bad." *Awfully* is an intensifier similar to *very*. Both are very informal and inappropriate for formal writing, but if you do use them, remember that linking verbs take the adjective, not the adverb. *Lamar feels awful today.*

being as, being that Both are colloquial for *since* or *because*. Avoid them in writing.

beside, besides *Beside* means "at the side of." *Sit beside me.* *Besides* means "in addition to." *Besides a trip to the Orient, he won $100,000.*

between, among *Between* expresses a relationship between two things, especially when they are thought of as individual units: *between the sisters*. *Among* expresses a relationship among three or more things: *among all the members*. Always say *between you and me*, not between you and I.

bring, take Bring a thing from a far place to a near one. Take a thing from a near place to a farther one. Think: bring here, take there. *Bring me my glasses and take this plate back to the kitchen.*

bunch A cluster of things, often growing together. *A bunch of grapes.* When applied to any mass, *a bunch of kids*, it is informal and not suited for formal writing.

bust, busted, broke *Bust* or *busted* are colloquial for the standard *break, broke, broken* or *burst*. Other meanings for *bust* such as "failure," "broke," "escaped," "jailed," "a punch," or "a demotion" are slang.

1. Between you and (I, me), this is a bore.
2. (Between, Among) the four of them, they didn't have a dime.
3. What time did you (awake, wake) me?
4. I plan to go off (somewhere, somewheres) by myself.
5. (Since, Being as) Taylor was ill, Hobbs subbed for him.
6. A (bunch, group) of people gathered in front of the store.
7. Gary just (busted, broke) a window.
8. Will you (bring, take) my books back to the library?
9. Her performance was (awful, awfully) (anyway, anyways).
10. Everett sat (beside, besides) Ernie at the fight.

Review

1. Will the new laws (affect, effect) your policy?
2. Your (analyzation, analysis) makes sense to me.
3. (Altogether, All together) now, recite the oath.
4. (Anyway, Anyways) you look at it, she's right.
5. Is that (all the farther, as far as) you can throw?
6. I want to think about it for (awhile, a while).
7. Bridget (an, and) Mac were married today.
8. The family divided the fortune (among, between) themselves.
9. You are (altogether, all together) correct.
10. Do you think the academy will (accept, except) women next year?
11. He (busted, broke) his watch playing football.
12. What would you (advice, advise)?
13. (Alright, All right)! Who took my shoe?
14. The boss (&, and) his brother are flying to Calcutta.
15. I don't know (as, that) I want to attend the meeting.
16. We picked (a lot, alot) of strawberries.

17. Please (bring, take) the rocker to Grandma's room.
18. I wasn't going (anywhere, anywheres).
19. (Being that, Because) I felt sick, we stayed home.
20. (Besides, Beside) Bart, who else is going?

CORRECTIONS

In a United Press International dispatch that appeared in The Times on Thursday, Representative Elizabeth Holtzman, Democrat of Brooklyn, was quoted as having said she would ask Congress to create a special council to protect the Government's interest in the tapes and papers of former President Richard M. Nixon. Miss Holtzman called for the creation of a special counsel.

The difference between a *council* and a *counsel* doesn't come across in speech, but it should be clear in writing. Do you understand why this correction was necessary?

choose, chose *Choose* rhymes with *cruise*. *Chose* is the past tense and rhymes with *close*. *If you choose the right number, you'll win a million. I chose black for this dress.*

conscience, conscious A *conscience* (n.) is your judgment of right and wrong. To be *conscious* of something is to be aware of it.

contractions Abbreviated forms in writing that mirror speech. They are appropriate in informal writing, but are seen occasionally in formal writing, especially where rhythms favor their use.

counsel, council A *council* is a group of people meeting for discussion. To *counsel* is the verb meaning to "advise." *Counsel* as a noun means "a lawyer" or "advice."

"Correction" © 1974 by The New York Times Company. Reprinted by permission.

different from, than *Different from* is always appropriate to formal writing, but if its use results in awkward sentence construction, use *different than,* especially before a clause. *The news was different than I expected.*

done, don't Nonstandard when used without an auxiliary. *He done it.* Nonstandard when used with third person. *He don't like milk.*

dosen't The wrong spelling for *doesn't* which is an abbreviation of *does not.*

drownded Wrong spelling of *drowned.*

effect, affect See *affect.*

except, accept See *accept.*

farther, further *Farther* refers to physical distance. *Further* expresses abstract ideas of advancement. *Let me say one further thing.* The superlatives are *farthest* and *furthest.*

fewer, less In formal English *less* is restricted to quantity—noncountables—and *fewer* to numbers—countable items: *fewer guns; less money.*

field, realm, area Often these words are superfluous. He excelled in the *area* of sports. In the *realm* of philosophy.

flunk Colloquial for *failed.* Inappropriate for formal writing.

freshman Only the singular *freshman* is used as the adjective form. The *freshman* class.

1. If you can't (choose, chose) a coat different (from, than) mine, don't buy one at all.
2. I almost (drowned, drownded) when the undertow became strong.
3. You do (fewer, less) work than anyone here.
4. This year we have (fewer, less) freshmen than last.
5. I only hope I won't (flunk, fail) composition.
6. The (freshmen, freshman) picnic was a success.
7. He is a whiz in (the field of math, math).
8. The (farther, further) you penetrate the woods, the thicker the underbrush.
9. He (done, did) his work carefully.
10. (Dosen't, doesn't) Terrence like lasagna?

good and   He got good and thirsty out there. Colloquial for *very*.

good, well   Interchangeable words when they describe health. *I feel good. I fell well.* However, they are different in other senses. *A good man. A well man.* When *well* is an adverb meaning "efficiently" or "prosperously," *good* as a substitute would be nonstandard. *He speaks well.*

gotten, got   Both are acceptable with the auxiliary *have*, but *gotten* is more common in America. *We've got a new house.* But, *She's gotten help from her neighbor.*

he, she, it   These pronouns should not be used after noun-subjects. *Meg likes books.* **not** *Meg, she likes books.*

had better, better   The first is standard for *ought* or *should*. *We better go* is colloquial and should be avoided in writing. *We'd better go.*

Page 64 discusses a similar error.

had of   Nonstandard. *I wish I hadn't of eaten that canape.* Change to *hadn't eaten.*

half a, a half, a half a   The first two are correct. The third unnecessarily repeats the *a* and is inappropriate in writing.

hanged, hung   *Hanged* is preferred for "to execute," as a person. *Hung* means "suspended," as a picture, though both are interchanged in speech.

hisself, theirself   Nonstandard for *himself* and *themselves*.

1. You (had better, better) get more sleep.
2. He turns corners (good, well).
3. Baker bought (a half, a half a) crate of grapefruit.
4. I've (got, gotten) dinner ready.
5. I wish I (had of, had) held my tongue.
6. Jeff was (good and, very) excited over the affair.
7. (Margot, she's; Margot's) a lovely person.
8. The gander preened (himself, hisself) constantly.
9. I don't feel (good, well) today.
10. Where do you want the picture (hanged, hung)?

if, whether   After such verbs as *ask, doubt, know, mind, remember, say, wonder,* use either. Where an alternative is expressed, *whether* is preferred. *I asked whether we should go or stay. I asked if we could leave.*

if you would have, if you had In an "if" clause, use *had* with the past participle verb form, not *would have*. *If I had been on time, I might not have missed the excitement.*

illusion See *allusion*.

imply, infer The speaker *implies*; the listener *infers*. *The story implies that he is in hiding. I infer that you are displeased with us.*

in regards to, with regards to Nonstandard for *in regard to*, and *with regard to*. Regards are greetings. *Give my regards to Broadway.*

inside of, outside of Less formal than *within* and *other than* for the sense of time and place. *We finished within an hour. Other than you, no one wants the candidacy.*

irregardless Nonstandard for *regardless*.

is when Nonstandard. The linking verb *be* should be followed by a noun or a structure functioning as a noun—a gerund, for instance.

See page 94 for gerunds.

1. Stealing is (when something is illegally taken, taking something illegally).
2. If you (would have, had) opened the window, you'd have had air.
3. Do not (infer, imply) my motives.
4. Send my (regard, regards) to Uncle Bob.
5. (Inside of, Within) two minutes, we'll know the winner.
6. (Regardless, Irregardless) of the weather, we'll go.
7. In (regard, regards) to your letter, my answer is yes.
8. (Outside of, Besides) you, no one else knows.
9. I don't know (if, whether) the amusement park will be crowded or not.
10. A fever is (where you burn up, a condition in which you burn up).

Review

1. The (freshmen, freshman) players have spirit.
2. What would you do if you had (got, gotten) a ticket?
3. In (regard, regards) to your order, the lamp is in.

4. She (implied, inferred) that she would be leaving soon.
5. Would you mind (if, whether) I come?
6. The child (drowned, drownded) in two inches of water.
7. The show must go on (irregardless, regardless) of interruptions.
8. A miracle is (when something extraordinary happens, something extraordinary taking place).
9. I refuse to walk one step (farther, further).
10. Does Angela regard herself as different (from, than) anyone else?
11. I can't decide (if, whether) I should dye this sweater.
12. When you (choose, chose) a book, consult the blurb.
13. If Ken (would have, had) dieted, his clothes would now fit.
14. I've spent (fewer, less) minutes on my housework since switching to Dustoff.
15. (Stella; Stella, she) needs thirty dollars.
16. Maxine plays the trumpet (good, well).
17. Rodrigo (had better, better) turn in his report today.
18. They give (theirself, themselves) all the advantages.
19. We'll need about (a half a, half a) loaf for the picnic.
20. (Outside of, Other than) the south field, I will inherit the entire property.

laid, lain See *lie*.
lay, lie See *lie*.
lead, led *Lead* which rhymes with *deed* is a verb meaning "to conduct." The noun *lead* which rhymes with *dead* means "a metal." *Led* is the past tense of *lead* and rhymes with *dead*.
learn, teach *Learn* is "to receive knowledge or skill." *I learned fractions in the fifth grade. Teach* is "to instruct." *I now teach fractions to fifth graders.*
leave, let *Leave* means "to depart" or "abandon." *Let* means "to permit." *Kim left for Detroit yesterday. Her husband let her travel alone. Let me alone* and *Leave me alone* are both correct. **Wrong:** *Leave me take the car.*
less, fewer See *fewer*.
let's A contraction for *let us. Us* following it is unnecessary. *Let's us go* is wrong; use only *Let's go.*

Transitive verbs are discussed on page 78.

lie, lay *Lie* means "to rest or recline," and never takes an object. Its principal parts are *lie, lay, have lain.* The past tense of *lie* is often confused with *lay*, which means "to put or place"; *lay* always takes an object. Its parts are *lay, laid, have laid.* He *laid* (put or placed) *the newspaper there.* He *lay* (reclined) *on the couch all morning.*

like, as These two words are becoming interchangeable in speech, but for writing, each still has a preferred use. *Like* is a preposition meaning "similar to." *She flits around like a butterfly.* As can be a preposition meaning "in the role of." *As a manager, he is a flop.* As is also a subordinating conjunction. If a clause (subject and verb) follows, use *as*, not *like*. *They left early, as they should.*

loose, lose *Loose* is an adjective meaning "not tight." *This tie is loose. Lose,* which rhymes with *fuse,* is always a verb meaning "to be deprived of." *If you lose this money, there is no more.*

lots, lots of Both these expressions are common in speech, but too informal for written work. **Speech:** *They have lots of noble ideals.* **Writing:** *They have many noble ideals.*

1. Jasper (lead, led) the hike.
2. (Let's, Let's us) begin to amble back.
3. Please (learn, teach) me to swim.
4. Will the doctor (let, leave) you go swimming yet?
5. He (lay, laid) in the sun all day yesterday.
6. Rick said he (lay, laid) the wallet right there.
7. (Like, As) Julie said, there is no excuse for this.
8. No one makes pizza (like, as) Tony.
9. I know (lots of, some) important people in the plant.
10. Did you (loose, lose) your boots again?

media The singular is *medium. Media* is plural. *Radio is a medium. The media (radio, newspapers, TV) ruined his chances for office.*

moral, morale *Moral* implies a sense of right and wrong; *morale* is a feeling of confidence.

most, almost *Almost* is an adverb. *We are almost there. Most* is the superlative of *more. He was most helpful.* In speech *most* is the colloquial short form of *almost.* In writing, *almost* is preferred. **Speech:** *An aspirin will cure most any pain.* **Writing:** *An aspirin will cure almost any pain.*

muchly Always incorrect for *much.*

myself Frowned on when used as a subject. *Both Ned and myself will be there.* As an object especially in compound constructions, it is acceptable for speech, but questionable in writing. Use *me* where it fits. *My pay supports my brother and me.*

never, not *Never* means "not ever" and should not be used where a single instance is meant. **no:** *I never saw you last night.* **yes:** *I didn't see you last night.*

number See *amount.*

numbers In formal writing, always write out numbers 1-99. Never begin a sentence with a figure. *Eighty men were lost.*

once and a while The correct expression is *once in a while.*

ought *Ought* does not need an auxiliary. Never use *had ought.*

outside of See *inside of.*

1. (17, Seventeen) people will be here for Thanksgiving.
2. I (most, almost) lost my mind that day.
3. The media (is, are) critical of injustice.
4. The gate receipts were (4,375, four thousand, three hundred and seventy-five).
5. Todd likes his new Kawasaki (muchly, very much).
6. Nick (never ate, didn't eat) breakfast this morning.
7. I like to dance (once and a while, once in a while).
8. Seth and (myself, I) voted negative.
9. When you find out, tell Zane and (me, myself).
10. We (ought, had ought) to buy a raffle ticket.

passed, past *Passed* is the past tense of *pass.* It means "did pass." *Past* means "beyond." *We passed the cemetery last night. It is past your bedtime. Past the shoeshop is the dairy dell. Did he walk past just now?*

prejudice, prejudiced Prejudice is a noun. *I have a prejudice against chocolate sodas.* It is also a regular verb: *prejudice, prejudiced, prejudiced. This book will prejudice you. I was prejudiced by that book.*

quite, quiet The two words are very different in meaning. Quite (adverb) means "rather." *She lives quite near me.* Quiet (adjective) means "undisturbed." *He had a quiet night.*

real, really Real is an adjective and in formal writing can modify only a noun. *Is that a real flower or is it plastic?* Really is the adverb that means "genuinely." *That was a really great play. I was really tired.*

See page 81.

reason is because Because is a conjunction that introduces adverb clauses. It should not follow forms of *be*, which require a predicate nominative. Substitute *that* for the conjunction. *The reason is that I was late.*

respectively, respectfully Respectively is used to show the order of two or more: *Smith, Barber and McGinnis ate oysters, clams and lobster respectively.* Respectfully means "with respect."

rise, raise Rise is an intransitive verb that never takes an object. Its principal parts are *rise, rose, risen. When will you rise tomorrow? I rose at six this morning.* Raise is a regular transitive verb that always takes an object. *Raise your head. I raised my hand three times.*

1. Karl is a (real, really) expert hog caller.

2. (Passed, Past) the gas station we (passed, past) an amusement park.

3. Jack and Jill carried an aluminum and a plastic pail (respectfully, respectively).

4. She is (quiet, quite) a girl.

5. Let the bread (rise, raise) two hours.

6. He (raised, rose) French poodles.

7. The reason he's upset is (because, that) he had a blowout.

8. We had a (quiet, quite) dinner together.

9. I am (prejudice, prejudiced) against that author.

Review

1. Are you (prejudice, prejudiced) against anything?
2. He soldered the connection with a little (led, lead).
3. Speak (respectively, respectfully) to your father.
4. The reason Giles came home was (because, that) he missed his parents.
5. Please (rise, raise) the shades, Sam.
6. He acts (as if, like) he's carrying a heavy burden.
7. Gordon and (I, myself) are going to the races.
8. There was (lots of, a good deal of) evidence to support his theory.
9. (Let, Leave) your keys here so that I can use them.
10. (50, Fifty) years ago, there was no TV.
11. Terrell has (lain, laid) on that bed for twenty years.
12. The media (is, are) influential.
13. We picked (4, four) candidates.
14. Nathan (most, almost) fainted when he saw the bill.
15. Come on, Neal, (let's, let's us) go.
16. The evening was noiseless, utterly (quite, quiet).
17. Will you (learn, teach) me logarithms?
18. Are you (real, really) tired?
19. When did you (loose, lose) your billfold?
20. Monica (passed, past) archaeology with flying colors.

says, said *Says* is often used incorrectly for *said*. *She stopped a policeman and says, "Where's Fourth Street?"*

seeing as how Nonstandard for *since* or *because*. *Since I was exhausted, I left the party early.*

sit, set *Sit* is an intransitive verb that never takes an object. Its principal parts are *sit, sat, have sat*. It means "to be seated." *Set* can be intransitive. *The sun sets.* It can be transitive. *Set the pitcher on the tray.* It means "to put firmly in a position." Its principal parts are *set, set, have set*.

somewheres See *anywheres*.

sure, surely In formal usage, *sure* is the adjective, *surely*, the adverb. **Writing:** *We are sure of a win. We surely don't belong here.* **Speech:** *We're sure proud of you.*

than, then *Than* is used for comparison. *Frieda is taller than Penny. Then* means "at that time" or "next." *He was a young man then. Then we went to the circus. Then* is not a coordinate conjunction. It cannot join two coordinate clauses.

that there, this here *There* and *here* are unnecessary in these expressions. Nonstandard: *Shelly bought that there pants suit.*

them as determiner Nonstandard. Substitute *those. Those children are out of order.*

this, that, for **very so** *This* and *that* are demonstrative pronouns, not intensifiers. **no:** *I didn't know he had grown this big.* **yes:** *. . . grown so big.*

1. The cat is (somewhere, somewheres) around here.
2. Bob will say yes, (seeing as how, because) he's in a good mood.
3. Peggy entered the dressing room and (says, said) "I'm a success!"
4. Rena is more patient (then, than) Patience.
5. Lena wants (that, that there) kind of ice cream.
6. (Them, Those) dishes have been (sitting, setting) in the sink all night.
7. I'd sit through it again, it was (that, so) good.
8. You (sure, surely) were good as Shylock, Brian.
9. Mary Quite Contrary is (sitting, setting) her plants three inches apart instead of six.
10. (Because we were winning, we went home; We were winning, so we went home.)

though, although *Though* and *although* are interchangeable. The spelling *altho* and *tho* are not acceptable for serious writing.

toward, towards *Toward* is the American form. *Towards* is chiefly British.

try and, be sure and Acceptable in speech but *try to* and *be sure to* are preferred for writing.

type *Of* is necessary in written constructions such as this: *This type of salesperson...* Often *type of* can be omitted without detriment to meaning. *That (type of) dessert tempts me.*

unique Some adjectives like *unique, perfect, round, circular, square* and *dead*, strictly speaking, have no comparative degree. The logical comparison would be, *more nearly round*. However, in informal use, *rounder, deader* and *more perfect* are acceptable.

used to Always include the *d* in *used* in the past tense. *We used to slide on a hill.*

wake, awake, waken See *awake*.

way, ways For writing, *way* is preferred to *ways* for distance. *He's a long way from home.* Other uses are colloquial and not suited to formal writing: *way back when, way past the bridge.*

well See *good*.

where for **that** Forms of *be* are followed by nouns, not adverbial clauses. Clauses should begin with *that*. *I read that three convicts escaped.*

whether See *if*.

Review punctuation on page 142.

which, that, who *That* and *who* are interchangeable as relative pronouns. *Is she the person who/that sold you this shirt? That* usually introduces necessary clauses. *The car that uses the least gas is my choice. Which* is never used to refer to persons. *The girls which I asked....* *Which* often introduces non-restrictive or unnecessary clauses. *The hot dog, which I bought at the Red Barn, cost sixty-five cents.*

1. It's a long (way, ways) home.
2. One thing (that, which) I hate is dirty socks.
3. We inched (toward, towards) the shack.
4. Why don't you (try and, try to) save your money?
5. I read in the paper (where, that) the garbage will be picked up on Thursday.
6. (Although, Tho) Viola felt well, she was weak.
7. The committee (which, who) works on gun control meets daily.
8. Tina painted a (more perfect, better) picture than Virginia.
9. When did you (use, used) to play hockey?
10. This (type, type of) student is a credit to the college.

Review

1. This (type, type of) test wears me out.
2. We fed the monkeys and the bears. (Then, Than) we visited the lionhouse.
3. Will you (try and, try to) make it tonight?
4. The children (which, who) live in that house are from New Guinea.
5. Put that money (toward, towards) a new car.
6. Rosalie (sit, set) the doll in the doll rocker.
7. As teenagers they (use, used) to dance South American dances.
8. Pearl settled for root beer (though, tho) she really preferred beer.
9. The bride was all the way up the aisle before she (says, said), "I've been framed!"
10. I see (where, that) the police will buy ten new squad cars.
11. The sugar maple house is just a short (way, ways) down the road.
12. (That, That there) necklace is the one I'll take.
13. She felt (sure, surely) about winning.
14. (Since, Seeing as how) Angie missed so much school, she decided to do the year over.
15. The cola company, (which, that) advertised selling sugar-free soda, was sued for false advertising.

MASTERY TEST

1. I will not (except, accept) you for the Glee Club.
2. The poem (affected, effected) her so powerfully that she sobbed.
3. When I returned from the bakery, I found that Mother had (already, all ready) done the baking.
4. Everything was (alright, all right) on the Western Front.
5. (Let's, Let's us) sing (all together, altogether).
6. I don't know (as, whether) I ought to go.

7. Room 111 is (beside, besides) 112.
8. She was different (from, than) the other actresses.
9. Kim (don't, doesn't, dosen't) like spinach.
10. The Smiths live (farther, further) in the country (than, then) the Browns.
11. We received no (further, farther) news about Dad this evening.
12. There were (fewer, less) people than we had expected.
13. It took (fewer, less) time than we thought.
14. He writes (good, well).
15. I (ought not, hadn't ought) to have done that.
16. (In regards to, in regard to) your question, I cannot make a statement.
17. It was (quiet, quite) monotonous work.
18. Will you (learn, teach) mc to read French?
19. (Leave, let) the car out in the rain; see if I care!
20. He (lay, laid) the gloves on the ledge yesterday.
21. This afternoon I (lay, laid) down for two hours.
22. I had just (laid, lain) down when the doorbell rang.
23. Did you (loose, lose) the money?
24. Ann and Emma ate an apple and an orange (respectfully, respectively).
25. Who donated all this money? Jack and (I, myself) did.
26. All of the girls (outside of, except) Mary were suitably dressed.
27. I have been (lying, laying) here for some time.
28. Give the money to Jim or (me, myself).
29. We're (real, really) proud of our team.
30. I enjoyed (that, that there) play very much.
31. She was a (very unique, unique) dresser.
32. He (raised, rose) petunias for a hobby.
33. I live a short (way, ways) down the block.
34. If you (would have, had) been here earlier, you would not have missed the bus.
35. We just (past, passed) the ford.
36. I read (where, that) gold will no longer back our currency.

37. (Being that, Since) you're working, let me bake the cake.
38. Bring whatever I'll need: slippers, robe, gown, (etc., and etc.)
39. What (affect, effect) did the movie have on you?
40. I ate (half a, a half a) basket of raspberries.
41. Which would you (choose, chose), Michelangelo or Moore?
42. The (freshmen, freshman) officers are here.
43. It looks (as if, like) it's going to rain.
44. Who (lead, led) you here?
45. The media (is, are) experts in persuasion.
46. If I seem nervous, the reason is (that, because) I just had an accident.
47. That book (most, almost) (prejudice, prejudiced) me for life.
48. It's so (quite, quiet) in here.
49. Your jokes aren't (all that, very) funny.
50. If you (try and, try to) master small points, your writing will (sure, surely) improve.

A DOZEN RULES FOR GOOD STYLE

Because style is personal to you, nobody else will write exactly as you do. While no one can say exactly how you should put words together, there are certain do's and don'ts that will determine whether your style is clear and logical or muddled and misleading. Here are twelve basic rules for good written style.

1. A pronoun should not have two possible antecedents.

Georgia gave Jeanne the message from her husband.

Whose husband is he—Georgia's or Jeanne's? Because *her* has two possible antecedents (words to which the pronoun refers), the sentence is confusing. The sentence should be rewritten to be clearer.

Jeanne's husband sent her a message through Georgia.

Rewrite each of these sentences to clear up any pronoun ambiguity.

1. Bernie told her mother that she had not heard from her sister for two years.
2. Whenever Sonny passes Gene on the street, he always greets him warmly.
3. The math professor told Skip that he would have to take a little time off to rest.
4. The dog nudged the cat aside and began eating its dinner.
5. If Ginny is Mabel's partner in the lab, she may pass the course.

2. Every pronoun must have a specific noun as its antecedent.

In school, they stressed the importance of spelling.

Who stressed the importance of spelling? *They* has no antecedent. Rewrite sentences like this one to add a specific noun.

> In school, Miss Thistlebottom stressed the importance of spelling.

Remember that a pronoun cannot refer to an adjective.

> **no** At the police station, they asked Myrna questions.
>
> **yes** At the station, the police asked Myrna questions.

A possessive word, even though it may be a noun, is modifying another noun; therefore, it cannot be the antecedent of a pronoun.

> **no** In O'Henry's stories, he always has a surprise ending.
>
> **yes** O'Henry's stories always have surprise endings.

Correct the pronoun reference errors in these sentences by rewriting the sentence.

1. Sable furs are expensive because these animals are small.
2. In this poem it states that death is hard to face.
3. After searching twenty minutes for Dr. Watson's office, Petra found him in the South Mall.
4. In Patricia's reminiscences, she often refers to her late grandmother.
5. In Eskimo communities, they travel by kayak.
6. At the beginning of the movie, it shows the villain in a sympathetic role.
7. In Dickens's books, he sometimes clusters verbs for a dynamic effect.
8. Swiss watches are reliable because these people are meticulous in their work.
9. As the test was about to start, they collected all our books.
10. At Jacob's house, he served us all tea.

> **3.** *This* or *that* **cannot refer to a chain of ideas.**

>> Jim's father published a magazine for ten years. Jim wants to do that, too.

According to the sentence, Jim wants to publish a magazine for only ten years. The sentence can be rewritten to eliminate the need for any pronoun reference.

> Jim's father published a magazine for ten years. Jim wants to be a publisher, too.

Change these sentences to avoid faulty pronoun reference.

1. Tina enjoys agriculture and has decided to take that up for life.
2. Martin joined the army before he was eighteen. That disturbed his family.
3. Dave was sick to his stomach and depressed. This was unusual for him.
4. You're having an early lunch so you can go shopping for new shoes. I think I'll do that too.
5. She has given away all her furniture and quit her job. This is so she can go abroad for a year.

> **4.** *Which* and *that* **(adjective) clauses must modify a specific noun, not an idea.**

> The cat fell into the fish tank, which frightened the fish.

What really frightened the fish was the cat falling in, but the *which* clause refers to the word *tank*. The sentence can be rewritten to eliminate the illogical reference.

> When the cat fell into the tank, the fish were frightened.

Rewrite each of these sentences to eliminate any illogical references.

1. She borrowed her mother's car which was a mistake.
2. Morris has memorized all the theorems which greatly surprised Ms. Black.
3. They turned the coat inside out which didn't seem to help.
4. Scoring a zero that he had never done before set Clark back.
5. They turned the lost wallet over to the store which they regretted later.

5. Do not use an adverb clause in place of a noun.

> Because you don't feel well doesn't mean you have to leave now.

The clause *Because you don't feel well* is an adverb, not a noun. It cannot be the subject of a sentence. Noun clauses never begin with subordinating conjunctions. The sentence should be rewritten to eliminate the adverb clause.

> The fact that you don't feel well doesn't mean you have to leave now.

See page 87 for a review of the three kinds of clauses.

Eliminate the incorrectly used adverb clauses in these sentences.

1. Over there is where we saw raccoon.
2. When he blanked out at the moment of the accident is the reason he didn't remember what happened.
3. An excuse for the crime is because the accused never had a stable home life.
4. When the Declaration of Independence was signed was the time when the liberty bell was cracked.
5. When you are ready to leave doesn't mean we all want to go.

> **6. Do not join the clauses of a compound sentence with *so*, *then* or *also*.**

We fed Trixie Cat Chow, then we tried Cat Chum.

Remember that the coordinating conjunctions are *and*, *but*, *or*, *for*, *either*, *neither* and *nor*. Only those six words can join the clauses of a compound sentence. This sentence can be changed to two sentences.

We fed Trixie Cat Chow. Then we tried Cat Chum.

Correct these sentences.

1. The old man liked beer and pretzels so I brought him some.
2. The astronaut opened the hatch, then he gingerly stepped out of the command module into outer space.
3. She wants eggs, butter and cheese, also she needs three kinds of crackers.
4. The score was tied in the last inning, but Ellen scored a home run, so we won the game.
5. The flag is red and white striped, also it has white stars on a blue field.

> **7. Use the active voice of the verb.**

Transitive verbs have a characteristic known as voice. Regular verbs are in the active voice. That means that the subject of the sentence is the performer of the action.

Marguerite kicked the ball.

When a verb is in the passive voice, the subject of the sentence receives the action. The performer of the action is often in a prepositional phrase beginning with the word *by*.

The ball was kicked by Marguerite.

or   The ball was kicked into the stands.

Although there are times when you will need to use the passive voice, your writing will be stronger if you can use the active voice.

These sentences are in the passive voice. Rewrite them in the active voice. You may have to create a subject or performer of the action.

1. I am insulted by that joke.
2. You were trained by the Maestro.
3. We have been visited by the Smiths.
4. The wicked witch has been pushed into the oven by Hansel and Gretel.
5. Otherwise they might have been killed.

It is important to use one or the other voice within a sentence.

When we got to the window, the strains of the piano could be heard more clearly.

The first verb in this sentence *got* is active; the second *could be heard* is passive. A sentence should be consistent, using either active or passive voice throughout. This sentence would be better in the active voice.

When we got to the window, we could hear the strains of the piano more clearly.

Make these sentences consistent.

1. As you approach the suburbs, flowering shrubs are seen in great abundance.
2. As soon as he understood that the president was displeased, plans were made to find another position.

3. The trees were blooming, the birds were singing, the grass was turning green and all the world had been awakened to new life.
4. Benjamin Franklin was accepted as a sage, and people enjoyed his wit.
5. You are admired for your honesty, but no one likes you.

8. Keep the same verb tense throughout a passage.

Edgar Bergen was a ventriloquist who makes Charlie McCarthy famous.

The first verb *was* is past tense; therefore, the second verb *makes* should be past tense, too.

Edgar Bergen was a ventriloquist who made Charlie McCarthy famous.

Rewrite these sentences repairing any inconsistencies of tense.

1. We are a hardy people who felt equal to the challenge of the wilderness in early America.
2. Indochina patiently suffered the ravages of war for ten years and builds a new economy in five.
3. The soap is advertised as organic, but everyone knows its main ingredient was a chemical.
4. Abigail Adams reminded her husband that he is essentially seeking to promote not himself, but the ideal of freedom.
5. I wanted to do a better job, but I know I've reached my peak.

9. Do not use more than one grammatical person to refer to the same thing.

Here is another case of consistency. If you begin with the first person (I, we), use it throughout. Do not switch to second (you) or third person (he, she, it, they).

When a man has done his best, you know it's time to quit.

This sentence switches from third person in the adverb clause, to second person in the main clause. A consistent sentence would be:

When a man has done his best, he knows it's time to quit.

or When you have done your best, you know it's time to quit.

Re-form these sentences to show consistent use of person.

1. If anyone strives for high ideals, you will be successful.
2. When the crowd cheers, we raise our voices to an unbearable pitch.
3. If you work eight hours a day, a person needs a rest.
4. In the navy everyone knows you must obey orders.
5. If anyone has change for a dollar, would you please stand up?

10. Express like ideas in like constructions.

The rabbit was white, furry and had long ears.

The like ideas in this sentence (description of the rabbit) should be written in the same form, in this case, as adjectives.

The rabbit was white, furry and long-eared.

Unless there is a good reason not to, keep the structures within a sentence parallel—in the same form—when they are expressing similar ideas. If you begin with a gerund, don't switch to infinitives.

no Stalking deer is more exciting than to hunt rabbits.

yes Stalking deer is more exciting than hunting rabbits.

A similar trap to avoid is mixing verbals and clauses. Be consistent.

> Knowing her and the fact that I don't want to are two reasons I won't help.

This sentence can be changed to two gerunds or two clauses.

> Knowing her and not wanting to are two reasons I won't help.
>
> or   Because I know her and because I don't want to, I won't help.

Correct these sentences.

1. The surgeon recommended swimming, playing tennis and to take a walk every day.
2. To think up a plot, to express it in an original way, to get a publisher to accept it and finally seeing it in print is every would-be writer's dream.
3. Children must learn to put their toys away and what time to come for dinner.
4. He bought two packages of corn flakes, three boxes of wheat germ and added on a pound of bacon.
5. Genevieve can sing, play the guitar and roller skating is another hobby she has.

One further thing to watch for is placement of correlative conjunctions. Correlative conjunctions come in pairs: *neither/nor, either/or, not only/but also*. These conjunctions must precede the same kinds of words of structures.

> Jill not only followed Jack uphill but also downhill.

The paired conjunctions must precede either two verbs or two adverbs.

Jill followed Jack not only uphill but also downhill.

or Jill not only followed Jack uphill, but also followed him down.

Re-phrase these sentences so that the correlative conjunctions fall before similar words or structures.

1. She not only wants a stereo but also a television set.
2. They cannot be reconciled because Jim will neither talk to her nor her mother.
3. Go swimming and either eat now or later.

11. Do not omit important words.

Don't make the mistake of thinking a small word isn't important. For example, if you omit the determiners before nouns in a series, a reader may interpret the nouns as referring to only one person.

no At the convention, I met a writer and teacher. (one person)

yes At the convention, I met a writer and a teacher. (two people)

A similar situation involves a preposition following a verb in a compound structure. Since the preposition can often change the meaning of the verb, it has an important function.

We were curious and interested in the project.

You can't be curious **in** something, only curious **about** it. The preposition must be included, too.

We were curious about and interested in the project.

Finally, don't omit the word that makes sense of comparisons between an individual person or thing and a class of things.

> Becky is taller than any member of her family.

Since Becky is a member of her family, she can't be taller than herself. To be logical the sentence must read:

> Becky is taller than any other member of her family.

Rewrite these sentences, correcting any omissions.

1. We were interested and agreed on the proposed plan.
2. We visited the baker, cobbler and winemaker in Jamestown.
3. Henry is younger than anyone in the office.
4. We asked the librarian for a newspaper and magazine.
5. The manager has specialized training and wide experience with work of this type.
6. A poet and publisher gave the keynote addresses.

12. Don't include unnecessary words.

Although prepositions that are part of idiomatic sentences must be included with the verb, your sensitivity to language should tell you that some adverbs are tacked on unnecessarily. If an adverb does not add to the meaning of the sentence, don't use it.

> Cover up the furniture so it doesn't get splashed with paint.

Covering up the furniture is no different from just *covering* it. The adverb *up* is not necessary and shouldn't be included.

> Cover the furniture so it doesn't get splashed with paint.

Which words could be omitted from these sentences?

1. The pearls were connected together by a nylon cord.
2. Look up Ron Jackson's record for me, will you?
3. Will you call me up Saturday?
4. Get off of your high horse.
5. I called to find out about how you are.
6. Continue on with your story, Grandad.
7. The polio left him crippled up.
8. Where are you going to?

Review

Make any corrections that are needed.

1. Clara's great aunt gave her a filly when she was very young.
2. According to Persian hospitality, they offer visitors fermented milk.
3. In Emily Dickinson's poems she uses slant rhyme.
4. Because his cousin wasted his inheritance at the races, Thornton decided not to do that with his share.
5. When Allen leaves shouldn't force us to go.
6. Timons joined the circus then he became a lion tamer.
7. Aunt Jane was made sick by poison mushrooms.
8. When Scott was stopped for speeding, they gave him a ticket.
9. If you try hard enough, a student can pass this course.
10. Thinking is not a bit easier than to go ahead and do something.
11. Before I grow too old, I would like to see a mountain, ocean and waterfall.
12. Let's reduce down by ten pounds.
13. Studying is beneficial to mind, heart and it makes getting a job easier.
14. We came, we saw and the enemy was conquered by us.
15. Thad felt dizzy so he went to bed.
16. Since you have a new transmission in your car, I hope you will use it more often.
17. He asked my age. I refused to answer that.

18. I offered to pay the man, but he would not take it.
19. Human beings are music makers. Where do we get it from?
20. I not only enjoyed the trip to the museum but also the picnic.
21. We bought a sofa, chair and loveseat.
22. The college neither offers oceanography nor geology.
23. ESP is building up scientific evidence every day, then it will be more widely recognized.
24. Rob knows how to knit, crochet, embroider and he can also weave.
25. Because you are tired is no reason to give up now.
26. In this book it says the Chinese have their own system of astrology.
27. Dr. Golden prefers Lowell to Dickinson which I cannot understand.
28. Please do not carry mud into the building. It makes the janitor angry.
29. I like hockey better than any sport.
30. Stanley settled in his favorite chair, then he flicked on the TV by remote control.
31. The requirements for membership were 1) scholarship, 2) leadership, 3) character and 4) being willing to serve.
32. They are willing to help, but they weren't very experienced.
33. When you have added up the scores, give them to me.
34. In Benjamin Franklin's lifetime, he accomplished many things.
35. When a driver passes another car, you can get in trouble.
36. Doing dishes, dusting furniture and to clean the house I can do without.
37. The boys hitched a ride to Philadelphia and boarded a bus which took two days.
38. She was fired from her job so she collected unemployment.
39. I am concerned and interested in your operation.
40. Knowing too much, this is her problem.
41. He constantly stirred the soup and opened the oven door which didn't make dinner any better.
42. When Wilma was recognized as a celebrity, she always leaves.
43. A copy of the memo was handed to me by Angelo.
44. Harold has already seen a lion, tiger and bear.

45. Rosamund asked Violet if she looked all right.
46. I love either a movie or hate it.
47. Open up this door!
48. Madeline knocked on the door, but no one was home, so there was no answer. That made her angry.
49. Carole Lombard was a star who was married to Clark Gable and died in an airplane crash.
50. Because you have gotten all these exercises right means you know a lot about English.

Do whatever is necessary to make these paragraphs read smoothly.

1. Every committee meeting reflects the heights and the depths of human nature, their nobility as well as its absurdity. There are always the agitators who, as soon as the meeting opens, have their hand up and mouth open ready to pour out his wisdom for the enlightenment of all, then there are the reactionaries whose only response seems to be "No," or "Let's wait." That has almost always driven the agitators insane. Between the two extremes are the indecisive ones. They swayed with every breeze. Because one is never sure of where the wishy-washy stand, is the reason that many issues are kept from being settled until the very last moment. If we want to get anything done, all three must work together in a good-willed give and take. You have to.

2. The framing of the Declaration of Independence was no simple matter. Thomas Jefferson, among the most literate of the members of the Second Continental Congress, takes more than a week to write it after discarding numerous drafts which had been considered by him inadequate. With the encouragement of John Adams and Benjamin Franklin, the other members of the Declaration committee, we now have a superb document which, in some persons' opinions, ranks in greatness next to the Magna Charta, England's guarantee of civil and political liberties established in 1215. Because the Congress questioned every word, phrase, and paragraph of the document did not hurt it but rather makes it stand the test of time. Think about it.

Cumulative Review

Rewrite this essay, observing the rules of style.

Astrology is daily growing more popular than any system of human analysis. Chinese astrology has twelve signs similar to the signs of the Western Zodiac. These signs are based on twelve animals which were said to have paid Buddha homage just before his death.

Unlike the Western Zodiac whose signs change by the month, the chief Oriental signs are arranged in a twelve-year cycle. Each year assumes the sign of one of the animals which follow in this order: Year of the Rat, of the Ox, of the Tiger, Rabbit, Dragon, Snake, of the Horse, Sheep, Monkey, Rooster, Dog and the Year of the Boar finishes the cycle. If you begin with the Year of the Rat in 1900, you figure all other years.

The physical characteristics of the animals have no relation to the persons born under their sign. For instance, persons who are born in the Year of the Rat (1900, 1912, 1924, etc.) are the most charming of the Oriental Zodiac. They are inventive, creative and have intuition.

Ox persons (born in 1901, 1913, 1925, etc.) are gentle and work well with their hands. They are usually successful also they can become violent.

Tiger traits include great sensitivity, to be thoughtful and suspicious. Persons born under this sign finish up luckiest in the Oriental Zodiac.

Persons born in the Year of the Rabbit or Hare tend to be talented, and have ambition and are discriminating. They are even, steady and melancholy people. That plus they have good taste.

Dragon persons excel in health, energy, honesty and courage, but they can be short-tempered, stubborn and with worrisome qualities, even so these persons live longer than other signs of the Oriental Zodiac.

In the classic book of Chinese astrology, it says that birth in the Year of the Snake not only forecasts wisdom but also vanity and selfishness. Although they overdo almost everything in life, these signs are sympathetic to others and never suffer financial problems which makes them agreeable companions.

Cheerfulness, talkativeness and being independent characterizes persons born during the Year of the Horse. They are full of wisdom, good in money matters, very impatient and hot-blooded in relations with others so they prefer to act on their own initiative rather than on advice.

Sheep persons are unusually intelligent and gentle, being sometimes too pessimistic. They have been outstanding in the arts and elegance is loved by them though you will notice that they are often unsure of themselves.

In the astrologer's view, he says cleverness, inventiveness and that they have originality belong to a person born under the sign of the Monkey. This makes them potentially good leaders. They possess common sense and are usually interested but not necessarily good at practical affairs, so they can become discouraged.

When children are born in the Year of the Rooster is the reason why we have persons who are enthusiastic, brave and love to meditate. Plagued by deep-rooted selfishness and eccentricity, these animal signs are the loners of the Oriental Zodiac.

In any Oriental astrology handbook, they claim that the sign of the Dog generates sincere and completely honest people which means they are original enough to be pathfinders. A bit stubborn, these persons make unyielding, loyal friends who know how to keep their cool, especially at critical moments.

The most mannerly and gallant of the Oriental Zodiac are those born under its last sign, the Boar. That produces people possessed of inner strength impossible to overcome, so they have tremendous staying power and make excellent students. Still, watch them closely. They can be impulsive, don't you agree?

Index

Accept, except, 178
Active voice, 200
Adapt, adopt, 178
Addition, edition, 178
Addresses
   capitalization, 127
   punctuation, 143
Adjective, 66, 80
   comparison of, 67
   inflections, 67
   use of comma, 139
Adjective clause, 87, 198
Adjective-forming suffixes, 24
Adverb, 70, 80
   joining, 85, 136
   unnecessary, 206
Adverb clause, 88, 199
Advice, advise, 178
Affect, effect, 178
Agreement
   pronoun, 114
   subject and verb, 102
Allusion, illusion, 178
Almanacs, 45
Among, between, 180
Amount, number, 179
Antecedent of pronoun, 114, 196
Antonym, 4
Apostrophe, 153
Appositive, 140
Archy and Mehitabel, 124
Art works
   capitalization, 130
   punctuation, 149
Article, 57
Articles (periodical)
   capitalization, 130
   punctuation, 151
Atlases, 45

Auxiliary, 62
   order of, 63
As, like, 187

Be, auxiliary, 63
Be, linking verb, 79
Biographical references, 47
Book titles, 1
   capitalization, 130
   punctuation, 149
Between, among, 180
Books of quotations, 46
Bring, take, 180

Capitalization, 124
   family relationships, 130
   letters, 125
   personal titles, 130
   poetry, 125
   proper nouns, 127
   publications, 130
Card catalogue, 44
Chosen, The, 1
Clause, 83
   adjective, 87, 198
   adverb, 88, 199
   dependent, 87
   independent, 83
   noun, 89
   parallelism of, 204
   punctuation of, 142
   relative, 111
Collective nouns, 107, 119
Colloquial usage, definition of, 41
Colon, 146, 157
Combining form, 5, 27
Comma, 157
   adjectives with, 139
   appositives, 140

Comma (continued)
  clarity, 141
  compound sentences, 83, 135
  conventional uses, 143
  identifiers, 140
  interrupters, 141
  introductory elements, 140
Comma splice, 86
Command sentence, 134
Common noun, 126
Comparison of adjectives, 67
Comparison with a class, 206
Complement of verb, 81
Complex sentence, 87
Compound object, 79
Compound predicate, 83
Compound predicate nominative, 81
Compound sentence, 82, 135, 200
Compound subject, 59, 103
Compound-complex sentence, 94
Conjunction
  coordinating, 83
  correlative, 118, 204
  subordinating, 88
Conscience, conscious, 182
Consistency
  of person, 202
  of tense, 202
Contraction, 154, 182, 186
Contrasting elements
  punctuation of, 142
Contrastive phrase, 99
Coordinating conjunction, 83, 135
Correction symbols, 218
Correlative conjunction, 117, 204
Counsel, council, 182
Courtesy request, 134

Dash, 147
Dates, punctuation of, 143
Demonstrative, 57
Demonstrative pronoun, 191
Determiner, 57

  before gerund, 96
  incorrect omissions of, 205
Dependent clause, 87
Dewey Decimal System, 44
Dialects, 42
Dialogue, 156
Dictionary use, 36
  encyclopedic information, 43
  idiomatic expressions, 39
  pronunciation, 36
  usage labels, 40
  variant meanings, 37
Different from, than, 183
Direct address, punctuation of, 142
Direct object, 78
Double negative error, 71
Dummy subject, 111

-*ed* form of verb, 61
Edition, addition, 178
Effect, affect, 178
Encyclopedias, 45
Except, accept, 178
Exclamation point, 134, 157

Fewer, less, 183
Field labels in dictionary, 42
First person, 202
Foreign words
  italicize, 150
  spelling of plurals, 173
Form classes, 59
Forms of *be,* 61
Fragment, sentence, 92, 98, 99

Gazeteer, 46
General and specific words, 3
Gender, 114
Gerund, 94
  parallelism, 203
Good, well, 184

Hanged, hung, 184

Have auxiliary, 62
Have-of error, 64
Hyphen, 151

Idiomatic expressions, 38
If, whether, 184
Illusion, allusion, 178
Illustrations, in dictionary, 39
Imply, infer, 185
Indefinite determiner, 57, 116
Indefinite pronoun, 58, 106, 115, 154
Indenting, 157
Index to Usage and Style, 177
Indirect question, 134
I Never Promised You a Rose Garden, 1
Infinitive, 94
   parallelism, 203
Infinitive phrase, 96
Inflection
   adjective, 67
   noun, 57
   verb, 61
Informal usage, definition of, 41
Intensifier, 71
Interrupter, punctuation of, 141
Intervening phrase, 112
Intransitive verb, 78
Introductory elements, punctuation of, 140
"Irregardless," 185
Irregular verbs, 61
Italics, 149

Joining adverb, 85, 136

Latin roots, 9
Less, fewer, 183
Let, leave, 186
Letters
   capitalization, 125
   punctuation, 143, 147
Library of Congress numbers, 44
Lie, lay, 187

Like, as, 187
Linking, verb, 80
Loose, lose, 187

Magazine titles
   capitalization, 130
   punctuation, 149
Microfilm, 52
Mobility of adverbs, 71
Modal auxiliary, 62
Modifier, 66
Motion picture titles
   capitalization, 130
   punctuation, 149

Negative, 71
New York Times Index, 52
Newspaper titles
   capitalization, 130
   punctuation, 149
Nonstandard usage, definition of, 41
Noun, 57, 126
   collective, 107
   inflections, 57, 153
   possessive, 153
Noun clause, 89
Noun-forming suffixes, 25
Noun marker, 57
   Negative, 71
Number, amount, 179
Number, of pronouns, 114
Number determiner, 57

Object, direct, 78
Object of preposition, 74
Object pronoun, 74, 78, 188
Omitted word
   error, 205
   punctuation, 141
Order of auxiliaries, 63

Paragraphing, 157
Parallelism, of verbals, 97

Parallelism, 203
Parentheses, 148
Participle, 94
   modifying noun, 69
Participle phrase, 73, 140
Parts of speech, 59
Passive voice, 201
Past participle form of verb, 62
Past tense form of verb, 61
Period, uses of, 134
Periodical Indexes, 48
Person, 202
Personal titles
   capitalization, 130
   punctuation, 143
Phrase
   adjective, 72
   adverb, 72
   contrastive, 99
   infinitive, 96
   intervening, 112
   participle, 73
   prepositional, 72
   verb, 63
Play titles
   capitalization, 130
   punctuation, 149
Plural of nouns, 57
Plural words, 109
Poetry
   capitalization, 125
   punctuation, 151
Possessive inflection, 57
Possessive noun, 153
Possessive pronoun, 57, 114
   before gerund, 96
Predicate, 77
Predicate adjective, 80
Predicate nominative, 80
Prefixes, 6, 15
   spelling, 170
Preposition, 64
   incorrect omission, 205
Prepositional phrase, 72, 96

Pronoun
   demonstrative, 91
   indefinite, 58
   negative, 71
   object, 74
   possessive, 57
   relative, 88, 119
   subject, 58, 184
Pronoun reference, 196
Pronunciation, in dictionary, 36
Proper noun, 126
   capitalization, 127
Publications
   capitalization, 130
   punctuation, 149
Punctuation, 133
   apostrophe, 153
   colon, 146
   comma, 135, 138, 141
   dash, 147
   dialogue, 156
   end marks, 134
   hyphen, 151
   italics, 149
   quotation marks, 151, 156
   semicolon, 136

Quantities, agreement with, 110
Question mark, 134, 157
Quite, quiet, 189
Quotation marks, 151, 156
Quotations, books of, 46

Reader's Guide to Periodical Literature, 48
Real, really, 189
Reference sources, 44
Reflexive pronoun, 188
Relative clause, agreement with 111
Relative pronoun, 88, 110
Resources, 35
Respectively, respectfully, 189
Rise, raise, 189

Root changes, 7
Root words, 6
Runon sentence, 86

-s form of verb, 61
Second person, 202
Semicolon, 83, 136, 157
Sentence
   compound, 82, 200
   compound-complex, 94
   runon, 86
   simple, 77
Sentence fragment, 92, 98, 99
Sentence structure, 56
Silent letters, 164
Simple form of verb, 62
Simple sentence, 77
Sit, set, 190
Slang usage, definition of, 41
Spelling, 162
   list of difficult words, 176
Statement, 134
Story titles
   capitalization, 130
   punctuation, 151
Style, rules for, 196
Subject, 56, 77
   compound, 59
   dummy, 111
   understood, 78
Subject pronoun, 58, 184
   after linking verb, 81
Subject-verb agreement, 102
Subordinating conjunction, 88
Substandard usage, definition of, 41
Suffix, 6, 23
   adjective-forming, 24
   noun-forming, 25
   spelling of, 165
   verb-forming, 23
Superlative form of adjective, 68
Synonym, 2

Take, bring, 180

Tense of verb, 62, 202
Than, then, 191
"The Latest Thing," 22, 60, 161, 175
Third person, 202
Third person singular verb, 61
Time, punctuation of, 147
Titles, 1, 151
   agreement with, 110
   capitalization, 130
   punctuation, 149
Transitional phrase, 140
Transitive verb, 78

Understood subject, 78
Unnecessary clause, punctuation of, 142
Usage labels in dictionary, 40

Variant meanings of words, 37
Verb, 61
   be, 79
   inflection of, 61
   intransitive, 78
   linking, 80
   tense of, 62, 202
   transitive, 78
   voice of, 200
Verb phrase, 63
Verb-forming suffix, 23
Verbal, 94
   parallelism of, 97
Vertical file, 51
Voice, of verb, 200
   consistency, 201

Well, good, 184
Whether, if, 184
Word division, 36, 151
Word order, vi
Works of art
   capitalization, 130
   punctuation, 149

Yearbooks, 45

Correction Symbols

1	**adj**	Use adjective instead of adverb (See pages 66, 80, 188, 189.)
2	**adv**	Use adverb instead of adjective (pages 70, 80, 188, 189)
3	**ag**	Agreement problem (page 102+)
4	**ant**	Antecedent of pronoun unclear (page 196)
5	**cap**	Use a capital letter (page 124+)
6	**conj**	Wrong conjunction (pages 83, 135, 180, 200)
7	**c s**	Comma splice (page 86)
8	**dic**	Error in word choice (pages 1, 35+, 64, 177+)
9	**frag**	Sentence fragment (pages 92, 99)
10	**ital**	Underline (page 149)
11	**l c**	Use lower case letter (page 124 +)
12	**p**	Punctuation error (page 133+)
13	**pro**	Wrong pronoun (pages 74, 79, 96, 114, 192)
14	**quot**	Error in use of quotation marks (page 151)
15	**rep**	Unjustified repetition (pages 191, 206)
16	**r s**	Run-on sentence (page 87)
17	**sp**	Misspelled word (page 162+)
18	**s s**	Error in sentence structure (pages 56+, 77+)
19	**v**	Error in verb tense (pages 61, 182, 186, 192)
20	**w o**	Write out, spell out
21	**//**	Use parallel structures (pages 97, 203)
22	**∧**	Insert something (page 205)
23	**⌇**	Take out something (page 206)
24	**¶**	Begin a new paragraph (page 157)
25	**O**	Other